The
FENG
SHUI
Garden

凤
水

*Design your garden
for health, wealth
and happiness*

Gill Hale

Consultant
Sue Minter
Curator Chelsea
Physic Garden

AURUM PRESS

*For my daughter, Caroline, and my parents for
their patience and support.*

First published in Great Britain in 1998 by
Aurum Press Ltd, 25 Bedford Avenue, London WC1B 3AT.

A catalogue record for this book is available from the British Library.

ISBN 1 85410 546 9

1 3 5 7 9 10 8 6 4 2

AN EDDISON•SADD EDITION
Edited, designed and produced by
Eddison Sadd Editions Limited
St Chad's House, 148 King's Cross Road
London WC1X 9DH

Phototypeset in Novarese ITC BT using QuarkXPress on Apple Macintosh
Origination by Pixel Tech Pte Ltd, Singapore
Printed and bound by C & C Offset Printing Company Ltd, Hong Kong

Contents

FOREWORD

There has been a veritable explosion of interest in Feng Shui in recent years, a far cry from the situation not so long ago, when it was almost unknown in the West. However, throughout the course of its meteoric rise in popularity there has been a vital 'missing link'. Gardens can make or break a property, and this book, at long last, addresses this fundamental aspect. People have always misunderstood the importance of a 'correct' garden: if a house is going to benefit from good overall Feng Shui, the garden cannot be left out.

In my association with Feng Shui practice, I had never focused on the significance of gardens in great detail, concentrating more on the shape of the garden and the plants it contained, or ought to contain. Then one day Gill volunteered to give a talk at The Feng Shui Association's Annual Meeting. We were expecting a general talk on gardens. As soon as Gill started talking, a hush descended on the large crowd. You could hear a pin drop. It proved mesmerising. At the end of the talk, everybody wanted to rush out and alter their gardening methods or get an allotment.

Gill's book contains everything you need to know about optimizing your garden and gardening methods to Feng Shui standards. Gardening is an extremely popular pastime around the world, but it has always been a source of amazement to me that there is a rather lemming-like attitude to gardening. Just as you can buy identical clothing to your friends or neighbours in a shopping mall, so you can buy an off-the-peg garden in a garden centre and, along with it, the means to foster the undesirable practice of spraying every moving thing with chemicals.

I have seen so many gardens with the lawn in the middle and flowers in rows on the sides, perhaps with a vegetable patch at the back. I find it astounding – and also quite sad – that the gardening methods advocated by Gill are not already in widespread use. It is such a logical and healthy way of going about designing and maintaining a garden, and the effort needed – if anything – is less than the 'conventional' chemical way.

The missing link is also concerned with the time element of Feng Shui. Time and plants? In Feng Shui, time determines who we are, who we get on with and where we feel comfortable. Plants have the same requirements. All around the world, the moon plays a critical role in everyday life. Some people only marry in a certain moon phase, for instance, while others may plan the birth of their child to coincide with an auspicious time. Moon-planting practices are universal, and have been for thousands of years. Surely this in itself serves to underline their significance?

Originally Feng Shui was concerned with living in harmony with the tangible and intangible forces of the natural world. The aim was survival and a reasonable lifestyle. Over time, other things have become associated with it. We hear that the number four is unlucky because it sounds like 'death' in the Chinese language. Of what significance is this in America or Germany? None. An orchid may symbolize endurance in China but something different elsewhere. Feng Shui is about living in harmony with *your own* environment, rather than trying to emulate surroundings that constitute 'good' Feng Shui elsewhere.

Feng Shui is ultimately simple. It needs no embellishments.

ARMEN ARTO
Brighton, Sussex 1997

INTRODUCTION

Feng Shui is a way of life which helps us to live in harmony with our environment. Having 'discovered' it on a trip to Hong Kong a number of years ago, I now have a much deeper understanding of why I intuitively garden the way I do. Feng Shui is a formula. You can spend years trying to crack the code and a whole lifetime yelling 'eureka!' as you continue to find answers to your questions. Feng Shui is viewing the world with different eyes. Ultimately it is very simple, but first you have to make the journey to develop the eyes to see.

ABOUT THIS BOOK

This book is not a comprehensive Feng Shui textbook; only the theory relevant to work in the garden is included. I have tried to retain the integrity of this great philosophy and its wisdom by returning to the principles on which it is based and leaving aside, where possible, the superstition and folklore that has become attached to it over the years. Although a Chinese 'system', Feng Shui is actually a way of life, and is applicable to us all. Every nation has its folklore, and its own symbols hold far more significance than those of a different culture. I hope to define the meanings behind the symbols, so we can choose the images that are right for us.

AN ANCIENT PHILOSOPHY

Ancient Chinese philosophers saw human beings as part of a natural order in which all living things on earth are affected by the movement of the sun and planets in the cosmos. It is a formula to unravel the meaning of life, the underlying theories of which are evident in cultures across the world. Uniquely, the Chinese recorded their knowledge thousands of years ago. This wisdom grew from observing the natural world and being aware of the intricate patterns that existed within it. Ancient peoples lived off the land, so any deviation from the natural order could have had a devastating effect on their well-being.

Modern societies have moved into cities and rely on others for their food, livelihood and learning. In our global society, few identify with one place, or have roots in a community linked by a common culture. There are, however, pockets of people who still retain a sense of place and community, such as those in the rainforests – people who take from the land and, in return, respect and care for it. In contrast, the developed world has taken control of the land and poisoned and polluted it. The world and its people are becoming sick. Our food, water and air are often full of harmful chemicals, and stress-related illnesses are common. At school, children learn about the effects of acid rain on buildings, about ecosystems and nutrition, and about pollution, desertification and loss of biodiversity, yet these topics are taught in different classes and rarely ever linked. Holism is not a subject on the curriculum.

THE 'WHOLE' VIEW

Some are beginning to question this way of life. In the early 1970s James Lovelock and Lynne Margulis formulated the concept of Gaia, taking the name from the ancient Greek earth goddess. They saw the world as a biosphere, a complex self-regulating organism in which every living thing has the same genetic code and thus a common ancestry. In other words, they viewed the world in much the same way as the ancient peoples had thousands of years ago. Those who work closely with nature form a unique attachment to the world around them. Fan Sheng Ching, author of an ancient agricultural manual, knew that it was time to plant beans when the elm trees flowered, and that lentils should be planted as the mulberries ripened, for example. Through observation of the qualities of various plants at different times in their life cycles, our ancestors knew how to use them for healing purposes. We are still using certain plants in this way today, and rediscovering remedies long since lost.

PERSONAL EXPERIENCE

In my early gardening days I learned a great deal from a neighbour who would tell me not to plant the onions near the beans and, from his observations of the moon and the stars, would tell me the best time to plant them. Such information was not in books at the time. Over the years, by trial and error and observation, I built up my knowledge. These days the information is much easier to find, and some useful references are included in the Bibliography (*see page* 125).

I regret not having access to my neighbour's diaries, which he kept for forty years, carefully recording weather conditions, the time that plants appeared and blossomed, the insect life at these particular times and more, much as Fan Sheng Ching had probably done centuries before. Yet, although the diaries would have been fascinating, they would not have brought the understanding which comes from doing. No amount of reading or listening to others' experiences can replace the true wisdom which comes from observing and connecting with your own space.

My recent studies have led me to Taoism, the ancient Chinese philosophy with its model of living which is still just as relevant 5000 years after it was first formulated; to acupuncture and acupressure, which use traditional methods to unblock energy channels in the body; to shiatsu massage; and to tai chi and chi kung, which use movement to aid the free flow of energy. I have learned about macrobiotic cooking and Chinese herbal medicine, which use ancient formulas to bring about health. I have become more sensitive to the energies that exist all around us and learned how to use my own energy to tune into the forces working in the earth. Feng Shui is all about harnessing these energies for our benefit.

THE RIGHT PLACE, THE RIGHT TIME

Feng Shui is about placing yourself in your environment in the right place at the right time. Chinese astrology tells us our favourable times, and which our favourable directions are at any given time. Ancient texts indicate prime sites with regard to terrain and watercourses. The healing arts show us how energy moves through the body and thus how to correct problems, and how food has its own energy which keeps the body healthy. However, I felt that something was missing. Surely this all-encompassing theory would have considered the correct growing conditions for this food which plays such an important part in the natural order of things, and the production of which was the daily occupation of ancient agrarian communities? As an organic gardener who also uses the passage of the moon to determine planting dates, it was inconceivable to me that the ancient philosophers who worked so closely with the energies of the earth and cosmos, and who were so meticulous in recording their wisdom, had not addressed the growing of their crops.

Everything has a time and a place, including plants. Documentary evidence exists in most cultures to indicate the use of companion- and moon-planting techniques, still used in rural communities worldwide. My research to date has shown that the Chinese used companion-planting techniques. They also used calendrical indicators based on solar and lunar cycles. The calendars were created at the Imperial Court and distributed to the provinces where they were venerated. Their interpretation has always been in the domain of astrologers and Feng Shui masters. The information contained in the *Wan Nien Li* – the 'Thousand Year Calendar' – which cross-references Chinese and Western calendars, has just become available in the West. I had planned some leisure time, but I know I will not rest until I have produced planting tables based on the Chinese system and compared them with the Western system which appears in this book.

I cannot help but wonder if illiterate peasant farmers living in China 5000 years ago – centuries before the invention of paper and efficient transport systems – would actually have had access to the information contained in the Imperial calendars. It is more likely that they would have used the same observational techniques as the rest of the world. Language barriers make access to this specialized information difficult. I would be grateful to receive any details of the use of moon-planting techniques in rural China.

FENG SHUI TODAY

Feng Shui offers us the chance to re-engage with the natural way. This does not mean that we have to return to the land and shun progress. In fact, the underlying principle behind Feng Shui is that change is inevitable. My studies have been worth it; an affirmation of what I believe to be the true path. The object of this book is to allow you to view the world with different eyes. If something appears to be wrong in your garden, do not look for a potion to put it right. Look for the cause instead, and then create the correct growing conditions. If your favourite fruit tree has a wound which will not heal, do not spray it, but look for rotting wood nearby which is harbouring the organisms whose roles in life are to break down rotting wood and recycle it into the earth. Remove the wood and the tree will recover. Simple, but it requires a different approach.

Recently I spent an hour watching a drama unfold. An ant, having overpowered a wasp, was propelling it along a path. How did it stun the wasp? Where were they going? Why did no other ant help? Then the telephone rang. I should have let it. When I returned, the drama was over and I will never know where they went. While technology connects us globally, few of us are connected to our environment. Time is something there is never enough of; we are never still and so rarely *see*.

There are signs of a new awakening. Calls for organic produce, sustainable energy systems, natural building materials and local economy schemes are no longer considered quirky. In New York, between the skyscrapers, community gardens are springing up on derelict plots as people seek to engage with the earth. We are gradually returning to the knowledge that we, the earth and every living thing on it are interconnected.

By observing the world around you and your immediate surroundings, you can begin to take control of your life and realize the patterns within it. By following the natural path you can indeed find health, wealth and happiness. Your concept of what these terms mean, however, will drastically alter as your understanding of this fascinating philosophy deepens. This book shows us how to reconnect with the forces and life processes on which our lives depend. Once we are aware of these, we can use them to create the lifestyles we desire.

GILL HALE
Croydon, London 1997

'There are those who lack respect
for the natural world;
awful things will happen to them.
Therefore respect where you dwell.'
LAO TZU, *Tao Te Ching*

Part One

Feng Shui Principles for the Garden

Understanding the ancient concepts of Feng Shui enables us to influence our lives positively and be open and adaptable to change.

Tao: The Way

'The way that can be spoken is not the real Way
The name that can be named is not the real name.'

LAO TZU, *Tao Te Ching*

These two lines from the *Tao Te Ching*, attributed to Lao Tzu, are the essence of a philosophy of life which has persisted through 5000 years of Chinese history – a philosophy that encourages us to develop the wisdom to follow the 'true' path through every aspect of our lives. It is a path based on nature and its cycles. It is understanding that there is a time and a place for everything within the natural world, and that to go against the natural way is to cause imbalance and disharmony. We cannot be taught the Way, we can only be guided to it. Current lifestyles and education make it infinitely more difficult for us to understand than it was for our ancestors, who lived closer to the natural world and depended upon it for their existence. Only by changing our perception can we begin to glimpse the wisdom within Lao Tzu's words. Following the Tao is to have a holistic view – to be able to predict the consequences of our actions, and to be adaptable and open to change.

THE TAO

It is generally accepted that Taoism evolved from as long ago as 8000 BC. Over time, many classic books were written, including the *Classic of Internal Medicine* ascribed to the Yellow Emperor, Huang Ti (c. 2697 BC), which remains the backbone of traditional Chinese medicine. Taoist wisdom was ostensibly written by Lao Tzu, or the 'Old Sage', who lived around 500 BC, although the philosophy of Taoism itself had already been in existence for thousands of years. The eighty-one paragraphs which make up the *Tao Te Ching* have subsequently formed the most-published book in the world. The underlying philosophy of the Tao pervades all aspects of Chinese culture: exercise, medicine, cooking, painting, calligraphy and astrology, to name but a few. It is the attempt of one civilization to make sense of the world, using imagery from its teacher, the natural world. The 'Great Beginning' resembles the creation theories from other cultures.

The Tao is not a religion and does not attempt to discover why things began, or search for a creator. The diagram (*left*) shows the foundation of this amazing philosophy, of which Feng Shui is a part.

Life emerged from the great 'emptiness', or 'void', from which the two polarities named yin and yang also emerged. This set up continuously flowing energies; indeed the two forces of yin and yang pervade the universe and ultimately give rise to all living things (*see also pages 14–15*). The fundamental aspect of Taoism that we

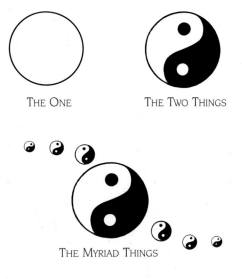

THE ONE   THE TWO THINGS

THE MYRIAD THINGS

'Tao gave birth to the One
The One gave birth to two things,
Then to three things, then to ten thousand ...'
LAO TZU, *Tao Te Ching*

Leonardo da Vinci's well-known symbol representing the trinity of heaven, earth and human beings.

need to recognize is that it is concerned with all life on earth, and views us as part of the whole order, positioned between heaven and earth.

SYMBOLS

Chinese culture is rich in legends and allegories, and its symbology has meanings on many levels. Its ancient wisdom, including its writing, is manifest in a form of shorthand or code. Circles, for example, symbolize heaven, and squares, earth; round and square openings are often included in buildings, garden walls and hedges, and such openings in a garden are known as Moon Gates.

Symbolically, Moon Gates enable us to see beyond our immediate space to the possibilities that lie ahead. At the beginning of the journey the code can be complex. We fill our minds with 'myriad things' as we journey down various paths in our search for meaning. By the end of the journey, our minds empty, we are able to sum up the meaning of life very simply.

LEFT. *Round or square openings, symbolizing heaven and earth, often feature in garden design, particularly in hedges or garden walls. They allow a view of the world beyond and, in Taoist thinking, open up infinite possibilities for movement and change.*

Yin and Yang

*'The mystical intercourse of yin and yang is
the root of universal life.'*

LAO TZU, *Tao Te Ching*

This renowned symbol is known as the *Tai Chi*. It is a mandala for contemplation, and it reveals the meaning of life on many levels. The circle represents the Ultimate Source, and within the circle the two forces of yin and yang are represented. They can be described as two magnetic poles, positive and negative, which are constantly interacting and creating movement. Together they create life.

Feng Shui is all about maintaining the balance between yin and yang. Each has the embryonic seed of the other within it. If one force reaches its extreme, it changes into the other. It is this very concept of change that is at the heart of Chinese philosophy. Take the following example of the interchange of yin and yang in the natural world.

In spring a tomato seed bursts forth from the ground (yang). It grows bigger as the growing season progresses (yang). Within the fruit small hard seeds are forming (yin). In autumn the plant shrivels and its life force and seed return to the earth (yin). In natural conditions, the hard seed remains dormant under the ground until the generative yang force in spring begins the cycle once more. These phases of the annual cycle are marked by festivals and celebrations worldwide.

YIN AND YANG IN THE GARDEN

The Chinese ascribe yin or yang qualities to individual plants. The begonia is particularly favoured since it is self-fertile and thus possesses qualities of both. It is by knowing the plants and observing their natures that we come to an understanding of the following essential concept.

Nothing in the natural world exists in isolation. In order to appreciate something light, there must be a notion of dark. Something tall must be seen in relation to something small in order for it to have meaning. The ancient *Yuan Ze* gardening manual indicates that the features in a garden should be balanced. Rough limestone rocks (yang), for

YIN: *The characters for both yin and yang depict a hill. Yin represents the shady side; a roof shelters the people beneath.*

YANG: *Yang represents the sunny side, although the sun's position will inevitably change, making this the shady side.*

ABOVE. *A form of shorthand (broken and unbroken lines) depicts the movement of the yin and yang energies through the seasons.*

RIGHT. *In this garden there is a balance of tall and short plants, of pale and dark colours and of light and shade. A broad-leaved plant in the foreground would improve the balance of the border.*

BELOW. *Fine-leaved plants are balanced by broad-leaved plants. This garden would feel very different if all the leaves were of a similar size and shape.*

example, are balanced by the smooth water (yin). Interpreting the symbols is crucial to the understanding of Feng Shui. The following pages show how the energetic patterns created by the interaction of yin and yang form the I *Ching* – the backbone of Feng Shui.

The Tai Chi symbol can also be used to represent the daily and lunar cycles as well as the cycle of human life (*see below*). Each quarter indicates a person's energy span rather than an exact amount of time. The lunar cycle is particularly important in terms of Feng Shui, as we will discover later on.

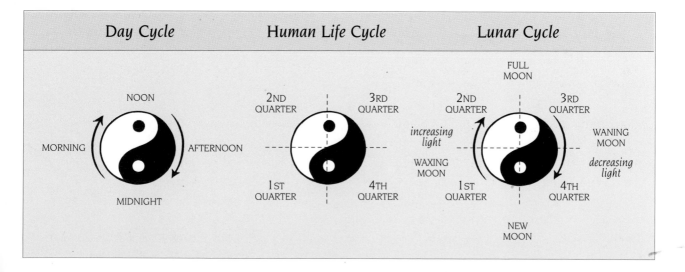

| Day Cycle | Human Life Cycle | Lunar Cycle |

Day Cycle: NOON, MORNING, AFTERNOON, MIDNIGHT

Human Life Cycle: 2ND QUARTER, 3RD QUARTER, 1ST QUARTER, 4TH QUARTER

Lunar Cycle: FULL MOON, 2ND QUARTER, 3RD QUARTER, *increasing light*, WAXING MOON, WANING MOON, *decreasing light*, 1ST QUARTER, 4TH QUARTER, NEW MOON

The Nature of the Energies

*Chinese language is symbolic, designed to evoke
an emotional response based on the sound of the
word and the image it conjures up. Metaphysical
interpretations at many levels of awareness
may be made for each symbol.*

The four types of energy which make up the solar, seasonal, daily, lunar and human life cycles are known as the Four Universal Energies. Ancient sages identified four further energies, some with yang qualities and some with yin qualities. These eight types of energy are known as the Eight Phases of Universal Energy and their interaction and interpretation form the backbone of Feng Shui.

Each type of energy is represented by a combination of three yin or yang lines known as trigrams. Each trigram was given a symbolic name, and by observing the positions of the yin and yang lines within the trigrams it is possible to see how each image arose. Heaven, for example, denotes nature at its peak; it is the masculine force, the sky, the cosmos, summer, full moon, noon. The image is of upward energy. Since heaven is the ultimate yang, it must give way to yin, and thus the trigram also indicates change.

THE STILL-LIFE PICTURE

The eight trigrams come together to form a sequence representing a universe in which everything is ordered and unchanging, and perfectly balanced. This is sometimes called the Ho Tu sequence, after the legend which suggests that the pattern of energies was revealed in the markings on the back of a dragon horse which rose out of the River Ho. More often, it is referred to as the Former Heaven sequence.

The Former Heaven arrangement is like a still-life photograph. Everything is in its place within a fixed order (*see diagram below*). In other words, it is a world where everything is predictable. The pattern according to the Former Heaven sequence allows no room for interaction and change, aspects that are so fundamental to Feng Shui. In time, the ancient sages found that this world-view was not practical: as soon as living things appear on the scene, the picture alters.

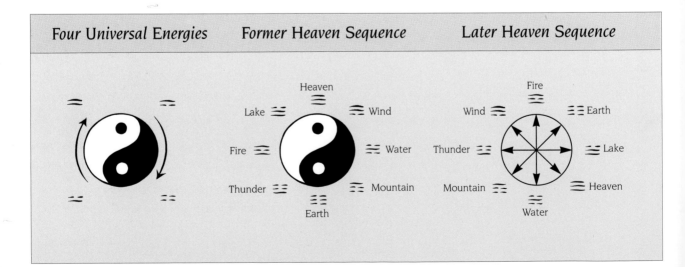

| Four Universal Energies | Former Heaven Sequence | Later Heaven Sequence |

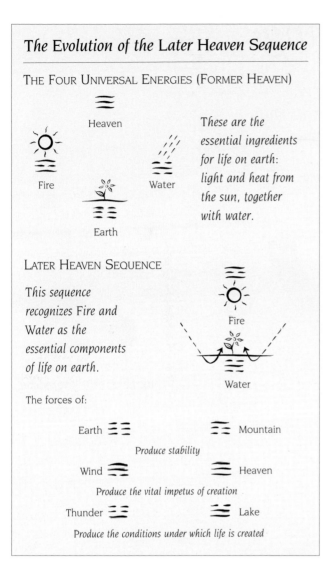

The Evolution of the Later Heaven Sequence

THE FOUR UNIVERSAL ENERGIES (FORMER HEAVEN)

Heaven

Fire

Water

Earth

These are the essential ingredients for life on earth: light and heat from the sun, together with water.

LATER HEAVEN SEQUENCE

This sequence recognizes Fire and Water as the essential components of life on earth.

Fire

Water

The forces of:

Earth — Mountain

Produce stability

Wind — Heaven

Produce the vital impetus of creation

Thunder — Lake

Produce the conditions under which life is created

A later legend tells of a tortoise arising out of the waters of the River Lo. The markings on the tortoise's back revealed another set of energies. These were interpreted as revealing the dynamic interaction of living things in nature. These energies form the Later Heaven sequence, also known as the Lo Shu sequence (*see diagram left*; transposed into dynamic opposites, the energies bring the world to life as the Later Heaven sequence).

The Later Heaven arrangement – the yang sequence of the trigrams – forms the basis for the *Bagua*, used to plot the movement of energy through a living environment, a house, office or landscape (*see pages 20–1 for more details*). The Former Heaven

sequence, since it shows a world at rest, is used for the siting of graves, particularly important in China as it is believed that the incorrect positioning of ancestors in their graves will seriously affect the fortunes of the family. This yin sequence appears on Bagua mirrors, which are often found hanging outside Chinese shops and restaurants to protect the building and ward off bad energies.

THE DYNAMIC PICTURE

The Later Heaven sequence shows a universe full of movement, but the movement is no longer cyclical. Each energy interacts with its opposite as shown in the diagram on page 16. The ancient philosophers gathered the information for this sequence from their observations of the natural world: for example, the interaction of Fire and Water brings about photosynthesis in the plant world, which is fundamental to all life on earth. It is a holistic view based on the interaction of living things and their dependence upon each other.

Since Galileo, scientists have believed that all natural phenomena are predictable and measurable. The Gaia hypothesis and the view of a growing body of enlightened scientists since the 1920s, after the discovery of subatomic particles, realizes that this is not the case, and that it is the very unpredictability of the patterns of nature which allow for development and change. In the garden, the mechanistic view would be to lament the presence of greenfly on the roses, develop a chemical formula for destroying the 'pest' and spray. Greenfly gone, a job well done. The new school – the deep ecology movement – would investigate the wisdom of planting a number of overbred hybrid plants susceptible to greenfly in the same bed, realizing that in destroying the greenfly we would also be destroying the ladybirds which feed off them. They would know that this would have a knock-on effect through the food-chain, that the micro-organisms in the soil might be damaged by fall-out spray, that birds might become sick, and the list goes on. Like Feng Shui, they view the world in a different way in order to achieve balance and harmony.

I Ching

*'If some years were added to my life I would give
fifty to the study of the I Ching and then I might
come to be without faults.'*

CONFUCIUS

In Feng Shui practice, the Eight Phases of Universal Energy are used to assess movement and flow of energy within an environment, but they are only a small part of a much larger picture.

Each of the trigrams – that is, the three-line representations of Fire, Earth, Lake, Heaven, Water, Mountain, Thunder and Wind discussed in the previous section – can be combined with each of the other trigrams to form a new type of energy. The diagram below shows how the trigrams combine to form the sixty-four hexagrams – the six-line representations of types of energy. The hexagrams form one ring of the *Luo Pan*, or Geomancer's Compass, which is discussed later on pages 54–5.

THE BOOK OF CHANGES

The sixty-four hexagrams form the basis of the I Ching, also known as the *Classic of Change*, or *Book of Changes*. It is one of the oldest philosophical books in the world, dating, in its present form, from the eleventh century BC. Familiarity with it is fundamental to a deeper understanding of Feng Shui. Over the centuries, philosophers have worked on interpreting the imagery of the hexagrams

and have assigned intricate meanings to each line and each hexagram. The movement of lines within each hexagram gives rise to yet more interpretations. Each hexagram represents the heavenly and earthly realms, with human beings in between (*see diagram opposite*).

CONSULTING THE I CHING

The I Ching is regarded as an oracle of great wisdom and power. It is not necessarily predictive, but offers sound advice in answer to the questions we put to it. The energy of the questioner and the question asked connects to it in such a way as to elicit a response which directs us to a course of action. The dynamic interaction of the energies of yin and yang, represented in their various combinations in the hexagrams of the I Ching, represent the patterns of the Tao.

The I Ching identifies the laws which regulate all natural phenomena, The emphasis is on change. Nothing is static in the natural world. If we go into the garden to plant a bulb and we pause to answer the telephone, on our return the world will have moved on. We may have missed slicing through a worm with our trowel, thus depriving a robin of some food. Perhaps

*Each trigram combines with itself and each
of the others to create the sixty-four energy
types, or hexagrams, of the I Ching.*

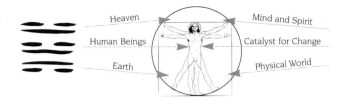

The top two lines of the hexagram relate to the heavenly realm, the bottom two lines relate to the earthly realm and the middle lines to human beings, the catalysts for change.

a squirrel might even have made off with the bulb. We can never recapture exactly the same moment.

The I Ching is consulted by casting yarrow stalks or, more usually these days, by casting coins. The way the stalks or coins fall in response to questions asked determine a yin or yang line. Each time the question Is asked, a further line is added until the hexagram is formed. Each hexagram represents a cosmic pattern of movement which suggests a correct course of action to be taken by the questioner. It provides advice which is as relevant today as it was centuries ago. There are many versions of the I Ching; every translation is different and the choice is a matter of personal preference.

INTERPRETING THE I CHING

Everything in Chinese philosophy may be interpreted on a number of levels. The hexagrams pick up on the theme of a spiritual and physical world – heaven and earth – with human beings constituting a changeable force acting between the two. We saw in the Former Heaven sequence of energies a still-life picture of nature, with everything in its correct place until human beings arrived on the scene. It is within the scope of human behaviour to interact with each other and everything else in the natural world in a positive or negative way. By way of a demonstration, here is a very modest attempt to interpret one of the hexagrams associated with Feng Shui.

The six lines shown in the diagram above form two trigrams – Water at the top and Wind (or Wood) underneath – and the image is that of a well. Once dug, if correctly maintained a well will continue to

provide water indefinitely. It is a stable fixture over the centuries. This stability is indicated by the yang line in the centre of each trigram. The water will be accessible, provided the means of drawing it up is reliable. If the rope is too short, the water cannot be reached, and if the bucket leaks, the water will be lost. In human life, the short rope might indicate that if people are too ambitious, they are unlikely to fulfil their aims. The leaking bucket indicates definite failure.

Let us consider a town council. The councillors are anxious to promote the town and, thus, their ambitions. They establish municipal gardens, with beautifully manicured lawns and colourful flowerbeds full of plants which are changed seasonally and are watered by sprinklers throughout the day. Important visitors to the town are always taken to the gardens to admire them. Yet in times of water shortages a hosepipe ban is placed on town residents, who occasionally also have to use a standpipe in the street when water is rationed. Pipes often leak badly but are not repaired, since the council and water authority dispute responsibility.

At its simplest, the image suggests that the town council is like a well. While maintaining a high-profile public image, it allows the Infrastructure to be stretched to breaking point for its residents. Ultimately it will be the council's undoing, since it will be voted out of office. The wisdom offered by the I Ching is that superior human beings should take care of those dependent upon them and inspire everyone to work together. Individual lines of the hexagram can be interpreted to offer further images and advice.

THE I CHING AND FENG SHUI

The ultimate aim of life, for those following the Way, is to achieve spiritual happiness whilst living harmoniously within the material world. The I Ching helps us to connect with our spiritual selves and offers solutions to difficulties encountered in day-to-day life. It has been described as a psychological computer. Tapping into it increases our understanding of Feng Shui and our sense of place.

Lo Shu and Bagua

*Magic squares exist in many ancient cultures
and are used as talismans. Very recently, some
of the ancient wisdom has been made more
accessible by its representation as the Bagua,
which enables us to harness the eight
Later Heaven energies.*

The movement of energy through the cosmos and through the environment affects every living organism on earth, and the object of Feng Shui is to harness that energy for their benefit. As we have seen, the ancient sages, from their observations of the natural world and the cosmos, charted the movement of the energies. As in all cultures, Chinese wisdom was passed from generation to generation orally through myths, legends and symbols in order to make it available for those who could interpret it. The patterns of these energies were, according to the legend, taken from the markings on the back of a horse and the back of a tortoise. One set of markings represented a still-life picture of the world, and the other the dynamic, ever-changing world in which we live.

We also saw how the energies have positive and negative qualities – yin and yang – which set up the dynamic motion of the pulsating, ever-changing universe, and how each of the Eight Universal Energies can be represented by one of the trigrams of the I Ching. The movement of these energies and the 'myriad things' they describe form the basis of the comprehensive and complex numerology which underlies the practice of Feng Shui.

THE MAGIC SQUARE

Each of the Eight Universal Energies may also be represented by a number, and the Magic Square represents the arrangement of the numbers. Its 'magic' quality arises from the fact that each line of three numbers – whether horizontal, vertical or diagonal – adds up to fifteen. In the West we are familiar with Magic Squares via the ancient Greeks. They are used as amulets in India, and in the Middle Ages were used in the West as protection against the plague, in the same way as the Chinese use the Former Heaven Bagua to ward off negative energies.

In countries throughout the world, complex theories were developed from interpreting the numerology which, in turn, grew out of interpretations of the patterns in existence in the natural world. The word 'geometry' simply combines *geo* (earth) and *metric* (measurement). Measurements from nature determined the proportions that were used in the design of sacred buildings and palaces and their gardens.

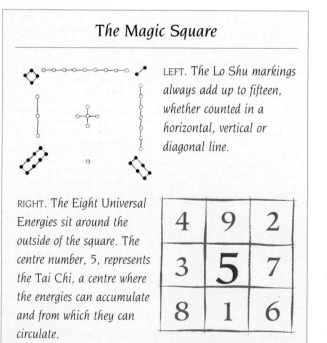

The Magic Square

LEFT. *The Lo Shu markings always add up to fifteen, whether counted in a horizontal, vertical or diagonal line.*

RIGHT. *The Eight Universal Energies sit around the outside of the square. The centre number, 5, represents the Tai Chi, a centre where the energies can accumulate and from which they can circulate.*

4	9	2
3	5	7
8	1	6

THE KNOWLEDGE OF KINGS

In ancient China, the knowledge gleaned from observations of the natural world and the cosmos was closely guarded by the emperor and the sages employed to interpret it. They had a saying, 'He who controls nature, governs the earth', and the emperors kept to themselves their understanding of the patterns of energy according to which they designed their living spaces and conducted their lives. By doing so they could retain their superiority and keep their enemies at bay, and also protect the knowledge of energy patterns from those who might misuse it. Such information undoubtedly also existed in the West. Who knows, for example, what lies hidden in the Vatican archives? Fortunately, in China, the information escaped various book burnings over the centuries, and is now freely available worldwide.

THE BAGUA

The Lo Shu, or Later Heaven, arrangement of the energies is used in Feng Shui to determine their passage through an environment, be it a home, a garden or even an office desk. The nine numbers on the Magic Square represent the Eight Universal Energies plus the centre, or holding force, around which the other energies move. This holding force keeps the energies in check. These numbers are called the Nine Palaces. Some Feng Shui practitioners investigate an environment by using the sequence of numbers on the Magic Square to ensure the energy is flowing smoothly (*see also page 55*). The arrangement of the energies has become known as the Bagua (or *Pa Kua*).

As we will see later, each number, or Palace, is associated with a colour, a trigram, a direction and one of the five elements. In recent years, names have been given to each section of the eight-sided Bagua to reflect a stage in life's journey. By laying a template of the Bagua over a particular environment it is possible to see if the energy in each section is beneficial and if it is in harmony with the other sections. You will find out more about this Part Two, when you discover how to use the Bagua as a design tool (*see pages 90–5*).

DIRECTION AND COLOUR

During the Ming Dynasty, nine temples were built outside the walls of the Forbidden City, to the south-east, to conform with the indications in the Zhou Dynasty classical texts. In 1541, just six years after they were completed, eight of the nine were burnt down in a terrible thunderstorm, leaving only the *She Ji Tan*, The Altar to the Soil and the Grains. The emperor viewed this as an omen – heaven's wrath at the vast amounts of money spent on the project – and the eight were not replaced. Is it perhaps significant that the altar at which sacrifices were made to the natural world for her bounty was the only one to remain intact – a reminder that what nature offers on the one hand is so easily removed if we stray from the true path?

The construction of the altar within the temple was symbolic. Square, to represent Earth, it was open to the heavens. On the altar were four triangles of different-coloured soils, one at each of the four cardinal directions, representing the provinces of China from which they came: red/south, green/east, white/west and black/north. In the centre was yellow soil from the area round the Imperial Court. The colours correspond with the position of the five elements on the Bagua, as we will soon discover.

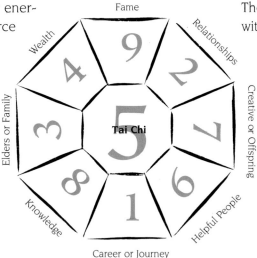

The nine numbers represent the Eight Universal Energies and a central holding force. The Bagua is used to gauge the passage of energies through an environment – a house, a garden or even a desk. The names allocated to each section express a stage in life's journey.

The Tao for Today

We are rediscovering ancient knowledge of nature's patterns, and accepting that nothing in science is fixed. By observing natural patterns we can begin to appreciate the movement of energy and the interrelationship of all things.

Scientists around the world are in the process of isolating every gene in the human body. Soon, the DNA map will be complete. We know that we share common DNA with all living organisms. Some scientists have commented that the structure of DNA and the pattern of the I Ching are identical. Both have a sixty-four-part structure and include linear and analogue systems which create complementary chaos or co-chaos. The emphasis is on change and constant movement. It seems as if we are on the brink of rediscovering an ancient knowledge.

Modern physicists suggest we are undergoing a 'paradigm shift'. Those with a less scientific approach may say that we are entering the Age of Aquarius. Whichever route we are taking, it is obvious that there is a movement away from the linear thinking of Newtonian science, which views the universe as a collection of unrelated objects that behave according to absolute rules. We are moving towards a less controlled view of a universe that is constantly changing, and in which everything is

As the water hits a stone it spirals out of control in a chaotic fashion before returning to its normal flow. Food dropped into a carp pond creates the same effect.

greater than the sum of its parts. The new view of the universe has order, but it is based on chance and probability.

Accurate weather predictions can become an obsession for gardeners. Since it is possible for the movement of an electron way out in the universe to affect weather systems, it is unlikely that we will ever be able to predict accurately. Gardeners in Britain often say, for example, 'It's snowing in New York – we'll be for it in a couple of weeks or so.' It is as accurate a prediction, but based on the observation of patterns.

CHAOS

In modern physics the universe is viewed as a vacuum, full of swirling energy. Chaos theory is based on the interacting positive and negative forces – that is, the relationship of yin and yang. One causes systems to spiral out of control and the other keeps them in check. In the Bible, 'the Spirit of God [wind] was moving over the face of the waters' (chaos) 'and there was light' (order). God created a perfect world, like the still-life, Former Heaven picture,

SPIRALLING CHI

The universe is full of swirling energy and potential chaos. The positive and negative forces, yin and yang, keep these energies in check.

and then introduced Eve, to stir things up a bit. In a similar way, some tribal groups have a trickster working among their gods to undercut the order.

FRACTALS

This moving energy can be seen in numerous guises: for example, the double-helix spiral of DNA, tornadoes, water draining out of a basin, the galaxy itself and in a flock of birds taking off from a tree. The patterns left in the natural world by the passage of this moving energy are called fractals, a term coined by Benoit Mandelbrot in the 1970s. Fractals are the patterns in snowflakes, rocks, leaves and tree bark. The splayed branches of *Cotoneaster horizontalis* and leafless tree canopies in winter are examples of fractal patterns. The patterns are repeatable, but no two are ever quite the same, since the energy which creates them is never still, but continually spiralling in time and space. Fractal patterns are created when the I Ching is questioned,

Drawn on a computer, the patterns on the cabbage leaves would be perfectly symmetrical. In nature, the patterns reveal a constantly changing world. The patterns are similar, but no two are identical.

but are never identically repeated if the same question is asked again, because time and circumstances have moved on.

A RETURN TO THE TAO

We seem to be moving closer to the Tao all the time. This does not mean we should all return to the land and forgo modern conveniences completely. Change is part of the system, and technology plays an essential role in creating the fractal patterns which gave rise to this 'new' theory. In order to move closer we need to accept that we are part of the whole natural order, and that we should not seek to 'control' it. If we try to control it, we upset the balance.

A return to the Tao will require a new way of thinking in all areas of life – economics, science and in the values of the societies in which we live. A closer cooperation with the 'myriad' organisms in the natural world will enable us to lead a more harmonious life. It will not be a simple journey, however. In the seventeenth century, Francis Bacon suggested that we should 'torture Nature' to force her to give up her secrets. Hopefully, in this Age of Aquarius, a new awareness is dawning.

In our role as gardener, working closely with the natural world, we can use our intuition to shun all processes which will unbalance the ecosystems in our gardens. For some of us it will be easy. For others it will take a little time to let go of the rules of control and accept the paradigm shift.

The Five Elements

'Nature has four seasons and five elements.
In order to grant a long life the four seasons and
the five elements store up the power of creation ...'

ILZA VEITH (Trans.), Nei Ching

The interaction of yin and yang, as we have seen, gave rise to the Eight Universal Energies, symbolized by the eight images from the natural world: Fire, Earth, Lake, Heaven, Water, Mountain, Thunder and Wind. In addition, the waxing and waning of yin and yang creates the five elements, or the five transformations of chi energy, which are symbolized by the five types of matter commonly found on earth: Wood, Fire, Earth, Metal and Water. Everything can be represented – and influenced – by one of the elements, from the seasons, directions and colours, to body organs, planets and shapes. In Feng Shui it is important for there to be a balance of the five elements, and this can be assessed by observing which elements are present. If there is too much of one type of energy, a place can feel disharmonious as a result.

In addition to the elements being balanced, they move in a particular sequence. The diagram to the right shows the natural progression of the elements, Wood, Fire, Earth, Metal and Water following the natural cycle. Earth is considered to be a transitory phase, from which everything originates and to which everything returns to be transformed into a new type of energy. Its obvious place is in the centre, but in the five-element cycle it always sits between Fire and Metal.

THE CREATIVE CYCLE

The Creative Cycle of the five elements (*below*) is also known as the Generative or Productive Cycle. The order of the elements in this cycle ensures that the energies of each element are in harmony with those of the other elements (*see box opposite for a useful way to remember the order*).

THE DESTRUCTIVE CYCLE

This is also known as the Degenerative Cycle. As can be seen from the diagram, an element can be threatened by another element which is two places away from it in the cycle. However, the order is not always negative. An element which is too strong may be controlled by the element which appears to attack it: for example, Water may reduce the impact of Fire, or Metal that of Wood (*see box opposite for a useful way to remember the order*).

ACHIEVING A BALANCE

The five elements have far-reaching correspondences (*see table opposite*). By observing which plants thrive in certain conditions we can begin to appreciate how the ancient philosophers built up their theories. Red plants such as salvias, pelargoniums and poppies, for example, are sun-loving and thrive in south-facing beds. Shade-tolerant plants which do well in a north-facing position, like *Fatsia japonica*, *Camellia japonica* and *Mahonia aquifolium*, have

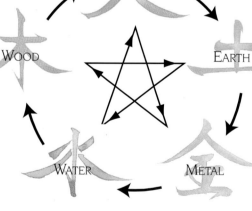

THE CREATIVE AND DESTRUCTIVE CYCLES
The circular movement of the energies shows the
Creative Cycle of the elements, and the
pentagram in the centre indicates the threatened
and threatening elements of the Destructive Cycle.

The Creative Order

• *Wood* feeds fire
• *Fire* burns to create ash or earth
• *Earth* contains metal
• *Metal* becomes molten and flows like water
• *Water* enables wood to grow

The Destructive Order

• *Wood* penetrates and feeds from the earth
• *Earth* soaks up water
• *Water* puts out fire
• *Fire* melts metal
• *Metal* cuts into wood

The Nature of the Elements

• *Wood* • denotes upward growth, like a tree or young shoot in spring. In life it represents growth, expansion and creativity.

• *Fire* • denotes energy and life at its fullest, radiating heat. In life it represents motivation and movement.

• *Earth* • denotes a nurturing, stable environment. In life it represents stasis – solid and reliable with little movement.

• *Metal* • denotes gathering and accumulation. In life it is associated with money and financial success.

• *Water* • denotes stillness on the one hand, and hidden depths and currents on the other. In life it is associated with communication and knowledge.

very dark blue-green leaves. The appearance and energy of a garden can be very different according to which element is dominant. As in Chinese medicine, a balance is necessary to achieve harmony.

An experienced Feng Shui practitioner will immediately observe if the elemental energies are not in harmony. It is possible to correct this by introducing the balancing element or elements. Examples of how this can be done for each element can be found on the following pages. The nature of the elements must be considered in order for us to understand their properties (*see box above right*).

THE FIVE ELEMENTS AND HEALTH

We are each affected by the particular energies emanating from the cosmos at the time of our birth. This makes us who we are, physically and emotionally, and also suggests which elemental type we are. Most of us are probably familiar with the Chinese astrological system, which allocates an animal to symbolize our year of birth. Each animal has an element associated with it, and it is possible to use plants of the appropriate colour or shape, or a container made from the material of the element if applicable, to benefit us. To find your animal and its corresponding element, refer to the table on page 124. The table of correspondences below indicates the colour and direction representing each of the different organs. By placing plants of our elemental colour in the appropriate direction in our garden or window box, it is possible to use the five-element cycles to focus on a particular part of the body. Please note, however, that this is in no way a substitute for seeking professional medical advice.

THE ELEMENTS AND THEIR CORRESPONDENCES

Elements	Colour	Season	Direction	Body Organ (yin)	Body Organ (yang)	Planet	Bagua Number
WOOD	green/blue	spring	east	liver	gall bladder	Jupiter	3, 4
FIRE	red	summer	south	heart	small intestine	Mars	9
EARTH	yellow/orange	midsummer	centre	spleen	stomach	Saturn	2, 5, 8
METAL	white/silver	autumn	west	lungs	large intestine	Venus	6, 7
WATER	blue/black	winter	north	kidneys	bladder	Mercury	1

LEFT. *The five elements have universal correspondences, the most relevant of which are included here. These can be used to focus on a particular part of our environment or body. We will come to the significance of the Bagua numbers later (see page 56).*

FENG SHUI PRINCIPLES FOR THE GARDEN

SHAPE AND COLOUR

Each element is associated with a shape as well as a colour. Too much of one shape or colour in the garden can cause an imbalance; we can use the Creative Cycle to create harmony. The elemental colours and shapes can also be used to focus on a particular area of the garden or, transcendentally, to focus on an aspect of personal life (*see pages* 90–5).

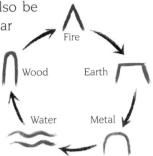

RIGHT. *The shapes and colours associated with the five elements.*

BELOW. *This garden is an example of the 'Too many colours' principle. Such planting would never be found in the natural world. The intensity of the mix of colours indeed 'blinds the eye'.*

'Too many colours blind the eye' is a saying attributed to Lao Tzu, and indicates that too many colours (or smells) can lead to sensory overload. In the garden below, for instance, we might admire the sheer quantity of plants and the gardener's dedication. Our next thought may be of the effort required to plant and maintain all these annual plants which are energy-consuming to produce and need a lot of water to survive. The hanging baskets need watering at least twice a day in hot weather to keep them healthy, and frequent dead-heading will be necessary.

We could never rest in this garden – there would always be a job to do. The garden will need constant spraying, since most of these plants are hybrid annuals and thus weak and sappy, attracting sucking insects. So, not a Feng Shui garden which mimics the natural world, but a classic example of human beings taking complete control of the environment.

～ WOOD ～

Wood symbolizes growth and expansion. It is flexible, yet strong. All growing things could be said to possess Wood energy. It is usually represented by columnar trees and structures. Wooden, rattan and wicker furniture, and wooden fences and decking, all belong to this element. Use the Control Cycle (*right*) to ensure that Wood is harmonious.

Shape It is rare to find the columnar Wood shape standing alone in the garden. It usually supports, or is supported by, another feature, such as wooden posts under pergolas, or brick pillars flanking gateways.
• **A** (*right*): Lone conifers look vulnerable, but they are overwhelmed if flanked by the Metal shape.
• **B** (*right*): Supported by the other elements, they can look majestic.

Colour It is amazing how many shades of green exist – and largely harmoniously so in a foliage garden. It is interesting to note that the pairing of green and yellow in variegated plant leaves (generally created with human help) does not sit well in the five-element cycle – a sign we should leave Nature to herself!

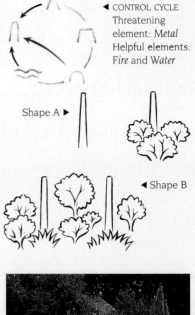

◀ CONTROL CYCLE
Threatening element: *Metal*
Helpful elements: *Fire* and *Water*

Shape A ▶

◀ Shape B

ABOVE. *These Wood-shaped trees will grow much taller. The surrounding plants will have to increase in size correspondingly in order to support the seemingly vulnerable and fragile trees.*

LEFT. *This lush green garden represents the Wood colour. Tiny specks of red give it interest, but do not detract from its verdant energy, yet sense of peace. This is close to the colours in the natural world.*

火 FIRE

Fire is hot and bright and moves upwards in jagged peaks. A garden with too much Fire is not restful. Its energy is overpowering and the colour too strong. Man-made materials represent the Fire element, as do lights and barbecues. Keep Fire harmonious using the Control Cycle (*right*).

Shape Fire-shaped wigwams are often used for supporting runner beans. Large numbers are traditionally grown in a row of wigwams secured by a horizontal pole, creating an Earth shape to temper the Fire.

• A (*right*): The wigwams and the Water-shaped planting beneath do not sit well together.
• B (*right*): A pole stabilizes the wigwams and creates an Earth shape to balance the plot.

Colour Splashes of red in long borders may be used to lead the eye forward slowly, but if a path is edged with red plants the motivation is to get to the end as quickly as possible! Red is a hot colour and goes well with the sun, although in cooler climates bright red is uncomfortable if there is too much in one place.

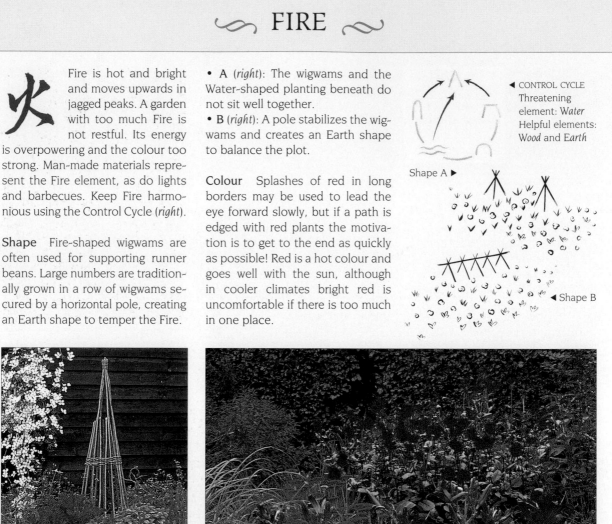

◀ CONTROL CYCLE
Threatening element: *Water*
Helpful elements: *Wood* and *Earth*

Shape A ▶

◀ Shape B

ABOVE. *The wigwam would be overwhelmed by the Water-shaped planting were it not for the support of the nearby trees (Wood) and the shed design (Earth).*

RIGHT. *Few people would feel comfortable spending too much time near this bed.*

EARTH

Flat-topped buildings, pergolas and fences, rectangular beds and straight-edged lawns are all examples of Earth shape. Earth materials include terracotta pots, rock, stones and brick. Use the Control Cycle (*below*) to ensure that Earth is harmonious.

Shape In the natural world, nothing is flat-topped, thus excessive pruning has no place in the Feng Shui garden. Birds, for instance, do not nest in regularly clipped hedges.
• A (*below*): The pergola and straight paths and beds are all examples of the Earth shape. The pergola is supported by Wood-shaped posts.
• B (*below*): Metal is introduced by creating an arch in the pergola and by introducing rounded bushy plants. Finials on the posts add Fire, and plants soften the path's edges.

Colour Yellow, orange and brown are Earth colours. Yellow in a border, particularly when used with white, can feel motionless; introducing red in the form of plants, a brick wall or a path can bring the border to life. Brown can be difficult, as it suggests decay. Orange and peach-coloured plants are lively in small groups, but their energy *en masse* is heavy.

RIGHT. *This rectangular pergola and path are typical of the Earth shape. The Fire-shaped leaves and decoration beneath the handrail, and rounded leaves of the vine, create a well-balanced design. The black Water colour does not go well, however.*

BELOW. *Not as heavy as some Earth plantings, these kerria flowers appear almost playful, which may indicate the plant's nature: it encroaches everywhere.*

◀ CONTROL CYCLE
Threatening element: *Wood*
Helpful elements: *Fire* and *Metal*

Shape A ▶

Shape B ▼

METAL

Metal symbolizes the process of gathering in. It is a dense, inward-moving energy, and it can feel oppressive if not in harmony with surrounding elements: large areas of white bedding plants can feel lifeless. Metal furniture, frames and fences represent this element. Use the Control Cycle (*below*) to ensure Metal is harmonious.

Shape In houses, Metal shapes (domed ceilings and archways) can seem as though they are bearing down. Walking through a metal-shaped plant tunnel or pergola can have the same effect.
• **A** (*below*): Walking down a path flanked by Metal-shaped conifers can be unsettling; in the dark they can feel as if they are closing in.
• **B** (*below*): A wide meandering path, Water-shaped, and a strategically placed Earth-shaped seat make all the difference.

Colour White and silver are the Metal colours. White plants can be very cooling inside a conservatory.

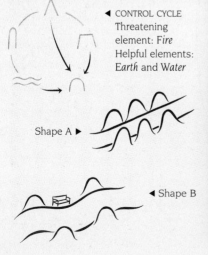

◄ CONTROL CYCLE
Threatening element: *Fire*
Helpful elements: *Earth* and *Water*

Shape A ►

◄ Shape B

Many silver-leaved plants tend to be low-growing and grow in drifts – the Water shape. Drifts of white snowdrops in a wood, for example, have an ethereal quality.

LEFT. *This domed feature is Metal-shaped. It sits well with the Earth-shaped lines of the fence and the shed roof.*

BELOW. *The Fire shape of the white lupins and leaves of the ornamental grass are in the Destructive order of elements. A more harmonious planting would replace the grass with some blue-green, round-leaved foliage plants, echoing the Water element.*

WATER

Water flows, meanders and creates waves. In the garden, the Water shape exists in meandering borders, in low planting in gravel beds and, of course, in rivers, streams and flowing water features. Ensure that Water is harmonious using the Control Cycle (*right*).

Shape The meandering Water shape can be easily created with plants, and it lends itself particularly well to gravel paths and the use of slate, which is often used to create a dry river-bed effect.

• **A** (*right*): The reflection in the water from this Earth-shaped bridge appears to cut the stream in half.
• **B** (*right*): The reflection of this Metal-shaped bridge in the water completes a circle – representing heaven – and is very auspicious in Feng Shui.

Colour Water colours are dark blue, dark grey and black. Too much use of dark planting schemes or materials such as slate can feel threatening, as can expanses of deep water, so it is best to temper the effect, using lighter tones here and there.

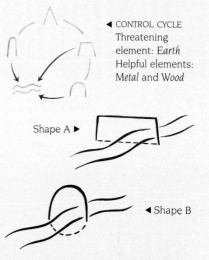

◄ CONTROL CYCLE
Threatening element: *Earth*
Helpful elements: *Metal* and *Wood*

Shape A ►

◄ Shape B

ABOVE. *Meandering Water shapes can be created with slate and gravel, and also by using plants in 'drift' formations.*

RIGHT. *The deep blue of the delphiniums is indicative of the Water colour, which could equally well be created with plants with blue-green leaves, such as hostas.*

Chi

*Chi is the invisible essential life force
present in every form of life in the universe.
Where it flows freely and accumulates,
there is health and abundance. Where it
stagnates, there is sickness and decay.*

Chi is not a concept that comes easily to the Western mind, yet it is a fundamental part of many cultures. In India it is *prana*, and *ki* in Japan. The Druids know it as *ether*. It has been described as dragon's breath, the life force, spirit, essence. Some have likened its movement to the flow of blood around the body. Yet none of these adequately describe the unseen subtle energy which spirals gently throughout the universe and through – and from – all objects, both animate and inanimate.

COSMIC CHI

Scientists have identified the existence of solar winds and lunar winds which move unseen around the earth. The biodynamic movement and native peoples use lunar, solar and planetary energies in order to determine the best times for planting and harvesting, as did ancient cultures around the world. Chi is present in weather systems and its effect has very different qualities, falling on our gardens as fine misty rain or as torrential rain, floating as a gentle morning mist or hanging as a heavy fog.

HUMAN CHI

Chi is present in each one of us. The Chinese believe that *jing*, tiny particles from the heavens, enter the womb and give the foetus the spark of life. A person's innate character is stamped upon them at birth, determined by the position of the stars and planets. In China, chi is believed to move around the body in energy channels called 'meridians'. When not flowing smoothly it can stagnate and create illnesses, and the ancient arts of acupuncture and acupressure are employed to unblock the meridians. In Chinese herbal medicine, particular elemental properties of herbs and other natural substances are used to restore the balance of the body, and the food consumed has to contain the essential life force. Therefore, the growing conditions of the plants and the way in which animals are killed is an essential part of the eating process, since, as the Yellow Emperor is reputed to have said, 'We eat medicine'.

EARTH CHI

Natural landforms have particular energies. In urban gardens, where mountains and lakes are not an issue, garden buildings and structures should be chosen to enhance the beneficial flow of chi. Plants build up a connection with the earth over time, and so long-lived plants, trees and shrubs are preferred to annuals, which are constantly being planted and torn up, a process that disturbs the ecosystem of the area. Nursery-grown annuals are expensive in terms of the global energy resources required to produce and transport them and the human resources required to maintain them.

Whatever we do in the garden in the way of altering natural landforms – uprooting ancient trees or diverting streams, for example – affects the energy. Earth chi is said to move through the dragon's veins. If disturbed, say, by cutting a road through a hillside, then the flow will be upset and disaster may follow. It may be, for example, that the road cuts through an established animal track, causing the animals to move away from their usual route. The removal of one species will almost certainly affect the balance of the area's

ABOVE. *Each plant and animal has its part to play in the ecosystem. We have yet to learn of most of the intricate relationships which make up the delicate balance between survival and extinction.*

BELOW. *Where chi flow becomes stuck and stagnates in a dark corner, a spiked plant can enliven the space and move the chi on. Such plants are not comfortable positioned too close to a seat, however.*

ecosystem, which, somewhere in the natural order, may perhaps cause a plague of another species.

Diverting the course of a river or steam can have a devastating effect on the environment, causing drought upstream and potential flooding downstream. Chi accumulates where two landforms meet, on the banks of rivers and in estuaries, at the base of mountains or in hedgerows.

Earth Energies in the Garden

We can encourage earth energies to gather in our gardens by addressing the qualities of yin and yang and the balance of the five elements, and by being aware of the qualities of the plants, structures and materials we use. Every component of the ecosystem of a garden is important, from the smallest micro-organism fixing the nitrogen in the roots of leguminous plants, to the largest oak tree, home to thousands of creatures. The chi will flow where they interact in a natural and harmonious way. Where there is imbalance and unnatural practices and forms, the chi will not flow smoothly and we will feel the effects of the imbalance.

A rock is so sturdy, yet reflected in a still pool seems to disappear into its dark depths. A still pool, for example, has a very different energy to a rippling stream. An ancient plum tree, with its gnarled trunk resembling a bent old man, has a different energy at its canopy, with its strong branches and delicate blossom.

However small the scale, we can introduce many concepts and energies into the garden. The stillness of a rock contrasts with the movement of clouds scudding across the sky; solid trunks with gently swaying bamboo; and the calm of a seat or summer house where we sit in quiet contemplation with the potential of a meandering path on which we may continue our journey.

The Feng Shui garden caters for the five senses – the smell of the blossom, the taste of the succulent fruit, the murmur of water and birdsong, the wonder of a single perfect flower and a longer view of the world beyond, and the touch of a craggy rock and a smooth pebble.

THE MOVEMENT OF CHI

By observing the natural environment, the ancient philosophers observed the movement of chi in the natural world. They discovered that chi curls and spirals through the environment, ebbing and flowing like the tides through each day, through the seasons and through the years. As we have already seen, chi can be either yang or yin in quality. Yang chi flows upwards and is a growing force, most active in the morning, on a daily basis, and in spring and summer, seasonally. Yin chi flows downwards and can create stagnant places. It is most active in the afternoon and in the autumn and winter.

CHI IN THE LANDSCAPE

Plants grow best where chi accumulates. In the natural environment this occurs where two natural features meet: for example at the edge of a pond, where earth meets water; at the edge of a border, where trees and shrubs provide shade and shelter for smaller plants which benefit from the increased light; and around a mixed hedge, where a variety of plants and wildlife create a supportive ecosystem. With worldwide deforestation, vast open plains have been created, across which chi gusts and disperses quickly. Such areas are usually dry and barren since the soil is rapidly eroded and chi moves very fast, rather than being able to accumulate.

CHI FLOW

Structures created by human beings deflect the chi from its natural path and force it to move unnaturally. Before building walls or hedges, or erecting any structure in the garden we should be aware of how the energy will move around that structure.

Walls, fences and solid hedges can create problems, since the chi hitting them is redirected, creating areas of turbulence on both sides. It is far better to have a woven fence or 'permeable' hedge through which the chi can flow freely (*see below*). Traditionally, such hedges were made from hawthorn with hazel wands woven through. In small gardens hedges can be created from plants in a shrub border, from flowering hedges such as escallonia and lavender, and from deciduous shrubs like *Corylus avellana* and forsythia. Likewise, trees and large shrubs with dense foliage can deflect chi, while those with a more open habit allow the chi to filter through.

Chi also moves through water. If you look at a pond, there are usually ripples on the surface and the water is in constant motion. A stagnant pond has no movement. If you have a pond like this, try to create an air flow over it through the surrounding plants. The term 'water' need not be taken literally. It can also mean 'flow' – the flow of pathways round the garden, or the edges of various types of ground cover – grass, paving or gravel.

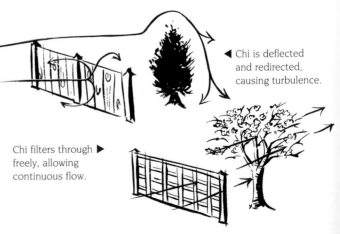

Chi is deflected and redirected, causing turbulence.

Chi filters through freely, allowing continuous flow.

Chi naturally moves in a meandering fashion, never in straight lines. It is worth noting that the permaculture movement (*see page* 64) recommends planting in keyhole and spiral beds which serve to maximize the flow of chi. By being aware of prevailing winds and the effects of various types of planting on the movement of chi, it is possible to plant in such a way as to harness the chi where required using permaculture methods and companion planting (*see page* 50). The different types of chi and their effects are discussed below, along with advice on how to encourage chi to accumulate.

SI: STAGNANT CHI

LEFT. *Cold air is heavier than warm air and, if trapped at the bottom of a hill or slope, it tends to create a frost pocket. These areas of stagnant chi usually feel cold and dank and not many plants are happy there. Likewise people living in such a place are likely to be ill. In this case it would be better to open up the tree or shrub belt at the bottom of the hill to allow the chi to flow through.*

SHA: CUTTING CHI

BELOW. *The straight top of the hedge, the straight brick walls, the straight edges of the lawn and the straight path are all funnelling chi far too quickly. Known as sha, this will create problems for the plants in the path of this chi. The space between the house, garage and side wall creates a funnel effect, the type of place where leaves endlessly spiral around.*

Flow of Chi

SHENG: BENEFICIAL CHI

LEFT. *The wind is now filtered through a looser planting, which is slightly higher on the right to take account of the prevailing winds. The open design of the front fence filters the chi, which gently meanders around the borders and the curved edges of the grass. A tall bushy shrub has been planted at the corner of the house to prevent the chi spiralling off the edge.*

Vibrational Energy

Living things are linked to each other and to the cosmos by vibrational energies, necessary for growth and survival. Harnessing them is the essence of Feng Shui. Disturbed energies can be detrimental. Our aim is to align ourselves and the plants in the garden to the auspicious vibrations.

The Chinese perceive a 'golden chain' linking everything in heaven and on earth. Homoeopathy, Bach Flower Remedies and biodynamic gardening techniques are all based on the theory that natural substances contain unique vibrational qualities. The biodynamic movement also uses cosmic vibrations to select the best times to grow different types of plants (*see page* 67). Those who 'talk' to plants are usually derided, but the vibrations have actually been shown to have a beneficial effect, in exactly the same way that insects, birds and animals brushing against them do.

HARNESSING COSMIC ENERGIES

The movement of the heavenly bodies has a profound effect on life on earth. They control the seasons, the daylight and the weather conditions, and their influences pour down on us to make us who we are. Later we will see how to harness these influences in the garden to enable us to grow our plants and our food in the most beneficial way.

EARTH ENERGIES

As the earth rotates on its axis, an electric current is set up within its crust which creates waves affecting all living things. The Chinese have known about electromagnetism since 2000 BC, and its effect on living organisms lies at the heart of Feng Shui. Natural disturbances can be brought about by a number of factors. Fault lines are one example, and underground water sources can have extremely negative effects on organisms living above them. Fault lines in the earth are known to dowsers as 'black streams', and underground water can dissolve particular minerals in the soil and cause the ground to become unstable. Recently in England, for example, an entire garden disappeared into a massive crater due to the underground water dissolving the gypsum in the rock beneath.

Scientists Dr Manfred Curry and Dr Ernst Hartmann separately identified grids of electrically charged energy which appear to run across the surface of the earth. One suggestion for the existence of these grids is that they are receptors for cosmic rays. The lines do not cause problems except occasionally where they cross.

Tunnelling and mining can cause disturbances in the earth. When the English first began to reside in Hong Kong they met with fierce opposition when they tried to penetrate the earth in any way. Telegraph poles were regarded as stakes being driven into the Dragon, and roads and railways were seen as cutting the Dragon's veins. The adverse

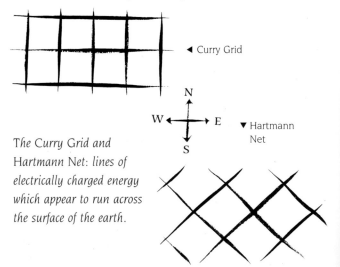

◄ Curry Grid

▼ Hartmann Net

The Curry Grid and Hartmann Net: lines of electrically charged energy which appear to run across the surface of the earth.

action of water, rays or human activity within the earth upon living organisms which reside above it is known as geopathic stress.

GEOPATHIC STRESS

Scientific research has shown that animals, including human beings, have a direct current linking them to the earth's current. Birds and animals migrate across the world and back, and in the past, when we were hunter-gatherers, we too found our way without the artificial aid of maps and compasses. Native peoples are still able to tune in to the vibrations of the land and know exactly where they are.

Living organisms depend on a stable earth frequency for their well-being and, where disturbances occur and the natural wavelength becomes distorted, problems will occur. Many Feng Shui practitioners use dowsing techniques to locate problem areas within an environment. There is evidence of dowsing in all ancient cultures. Many people can simply *sense* geopathic stress. A place may feel dull or heavy, or cold. In a garden there are visible clues: some plants actually thrive on geopathic stress, as do some animals.

The presence of the stress seekers does not necessarily mean that geopathic stress is present in the garden, but a cat's favourite sleeping place is one indicator of its possible presence. In my

STRESS SEEKERS AND AVOIDERS

ORGANISM	STRESS SEEKERS	STRESS AVOIDERS
Animal	Ants Bacteria Bees and Wasps Beetles Cats	Birds Chickens Dogs Fish Horses
Plant	Asparagus Cherry Elder Garrya elliptica Mushrooms Oak Plum Willow	Apple Azaleas Celery Onions Pear Privet Pyracantha Sunflowers

own garden, elder trees flourish along one particular border. As an organic gardener, this is where I locate the compost heaps, since it is well known that elder roots growing through compost cause it to break down much more quickly to produce sweet-smelling, crumbly compost. It is interesting to note that the micro-organisms which break down organic materials also thrive on geopathic stress. Another useful indicator in my garden is the presence of stag beetles, now an endangered species, but thriving in my compost bins!

We are advised never to shelter under an oak tree during a storm. This is sound advice. Oaks thrive where two underground streams cross, thus creating a disturbance in the earth's electromagnetic field which attracts the electromagnetic energy of the storm – lightning. Another indicator of geopathic stress in the garden is a bed where trees and shrubs seem to be bending in a certain direction. If they are not bending towards the light, or because of a prevailing wind, the chances are they are attempting to avoid the stress.

Trees with cancerous growths on their trunks are indicative, and fruit trees which fail to set fruit may also signal stress, but first check on more obvious solutions, like the absence of pollinating insects. If you grow vegetables which tend to rot in storage, your shed or garage may well be located on a stress line.

LEFT. *If plants are distressed for no obvious reason, then geopathic stress may well be the cause.*

RIGHT. *Healthy plants need the correct aspect and type of soil, and healthy growing conditions to thrive.*

The Right Time and Place: People

The concepts of time and place are an integral part of Feng Shui. We are all stamped with a cosmic imprint at our moment of birth which determines our character, fortune and destiny. Houses, too, pick up the cosmic energies present when they are built or extended.

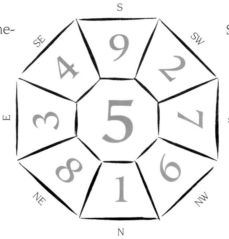

*Since Chinese astrologers read the skies facing the equator, south is written where we expect north to be. The directions as read from an ordinary magnetic compass are not affected: do **not** try to reverse them.*

Chinese astrology is extremely complex. The calendar is lunar – that is, every month begins with a new moon, which is why the Chinese new year falls at different times between mid-January and mid-February. In Feng Shui, however, calculations are based on the solar calendar. The time components of the subject the auspicious times to build, to move or to begin a project – take both lunar and solar cycles into consideration and involve lengthy calculations, since, as yet, the Chinese almanacs have not been translated for use outside the Chinese-speaking community. A number of different systems can be used to determine beneficial locations for houses and their occupants, and Feng Shui practitioners will use a particular system based on personal preference or the situation that they are addressing. Most use more than one. In some systems it is possible to choose correct locations over a period of time since, as we have seen, nothing is fixed and we live in a world of constant change.

BENEFICIAL LOCATIONS

According to astrological calculations, the time when a house was built or the time when a person was born determines the best location for them.

Sometimes the houses we live in are not situated in a favourable location for us. Inside the house we can rectify this to some extent by choosing to sleep and work in rooms within our favourable location. In the garden, a workshop or office extension, or perhaps a summer house or favourite seat, can be placed in a beneficial location.

For the purposes of this book, the methods used are based on the theory already covered. Once you have found which direction your house faces and its corresponding element, and your own favoured direction with its corresponding element, you can then use the five-element cycles (*see pages* 24–31) to create a comfortable leisure or work space in the garden.

TO FIND THE HOUSE DIRECTION

An ordinary magnetic compass is required for this. Follow the steps below.

1. Remove watches, jewellery and any metal items from your clothing. These objects may affect the compass.
2. Stand outside the house, facing away from it.
3. Check if any metal objects are nearby – doors, furniture, cars, metal planters, for example – and move away from them.

4. The needle of the compass will align itself in a north–south direction. Move the compass around until the north and south markings are at either end of the compass needle. The direction your house faces will be the direction pointing away from you on the compass face.

TO FIND THE HOUSE ELEMENT

Once the house direction is known, consult the House Element table (*below*) to find out which element corresponds to the direction.

TO FIND YOUR PERSONAL ELEMENT AND DIRECTION

1. Use the Year Number table (*right*) to find the number for your year of birth. Since the solar new year begins on the fourth or fifth of February each year, if your birth date falls before this use the number for the previous year for these calculations (*see page 124 for solar new year dates*). (NOTE: there are different numbers for males (M) and females (F).)

It may be worth noting here that some practitioners use the same number for males and females. Another approach suggests that, since females are increasingly becoming more yang in their daily lives, the male number represents ourselves as we appear to the world and the female number represents our inner selves.

YEAR NUMBER											
YEAR	M	F	YEAR	M	F	YEAR	M	F	YEAR	M	F
1924	4	2	1945	1	5	1966	7	8	1987	4	2
1925	3	3	1946	9	6	1967	6	9	1988	3	3
1926	2	4	1947	8	7	1968	5	1	1989	2	4
1927	1	5	1948	7	8	1969	4	2	1990	1	5
1928	9	6	1949	6	9	1970	3	3	1991	9	6
1929	8	7	1950	5	1	1971	2	4	1992	8	7
1930	7	8	1951	4	2	1972	1	5	1993	7	8
1931	6	9	1952	3	3	1973	9	6	1994	6	9
1932	5	1	1953	2	4	1974	8	7	1995	5	1
1933	4	2	1954	1	5	1975	7	8	1996	4	2
1934	3	3	1955	9	6	1976	6	9	1997	3	3
1935	2	4	1956	8	7	1977	5	1	1998	2	4
1936	1	5	1957	7	8	1978	4	2	1999	1	5
1937	9	6	1958	6	9	1979	3	3	2000	9	6
1938	8	7	1959	5	1	1980	2	4	2001	8	7
1939	7	8	1960	4	2	1981	1	5	2002	7	8
1940	6	9	1961	3	3	1982	9	6	2003	6	9
1941	5	1	1962	2	4	1983	8	7	2004	5	1
1942	4	2	1963	1	5	1984	7	8	2005	4	2
1943	3	3	1964	9	6	1985	6	9	2006	3	3
1944	2	4	1965	8	7	1986	5	1	2007	2	4

2. Find your year number in the Personal Element and Direction table (*see below left*) to find out your personal element and the best direction for you to face. We have already seen in the section on the Lo Shu and Bagua (*pages 20–1*) that the number 5 takes a central position and therefore does not correspond to one of the eight directions. It corresponds to the Earth element, as do the numbers 2 and 8. For the purposes of finding directions in Feng Shui, when the personal number is number 5, males are assigned the characteristics of number 2 and thus the south-west direction, and females number 8 and the north-east. Number 5 still remains the year number for other purposes.

HOUSE ELEMENT		PERSONAL ELEMENT AND DIRECTION		
Direction	Element	Year No.	Element	Best Direction
south	Fire	1	Water	*north*
south-east	Wood	2	Earth	*south-west*
east	Wood	3	Wood	*east*
north-east	Earth	4	Wood	*south-east*
north	Water	5	Earth	*south-west* (M)
north-west	Metal			*north-east* (F)
west	Metal	6	Metal	*north-west*
south-west	Earth	7	Metal	*west*
		8	Earth	*north-east*
		9	Fire	*south*

Example

If a house faces east, it belongs to the Wood element. Since Water feeds Wood in the five-element cycle, a water feature or low meandering planting could be introduced. Some Fire-shaped finials on the gateposts would ensure that the elements are balanced. If the person living in the house is a female born in 1951 (on 4 February or later), then her personal number is 2 – an Earth number, with the direction of south-west. Therefore a seat placed to face south-west, opposite a terracotta urn representing the Earth element, and supported by some Fire and Metal, would make an ideal spot.

The Right Time: Plants

'For everything there is a season
and a time for every purpose under heaven;
a time to be born, and a time to die,
a time to plant and a time to pluck up
what is planted ...'

Ecclesiastes 3, 1–2

Plants, like people, respond to their environment. All rural dwellers, until fairly recently, were very specific in their planting times. It was crucial that the plants were given the best possible conditions, since the lives of the community depended on a successful harvest. With no clocks or calendars available, our predecessors relied on the movement of the heavenly bodies in order to determine the best times for sowing, tending and nurturing their crops.

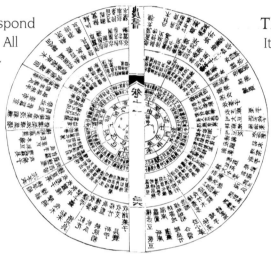

This agricultural calendar from Wang Chen's Nung Shu *of* AD 1313 *identifies natural phenomena and shows seasonal and climatic periods, indicating the correct times for agricultural tasks to be undertaken.*

Various systems were used to determine the best crop-planting times in ancient China. One used the blossoming times of various plants and trees. The manual, the *Huai Nan Tzu*, used the position of the constellations. *The Book of Fan Sheng Ching*, from the first century BC, gives very precise instructions based on the solar calendar, recommending that rice should be sown 110 days after the winter solstice. The *Chhi Min Yao Shu* (Essential Techniques for the Peasantry), dated AD 535, is based on the lunar calendar, and recommended the planting of spring soya beans in the second *hsun* (ten-day period) of the second month, and the next best time for planting small beans was 'just before dog days'!

THE SOLAR CALENDAR

It is reported that in 2698 BC, Huang Ti, the Yellow Emperor, instigated a solar calendar based on the accumulated knowledge of the sages who had studied the natural cycle. This calendar shows the year divided into twenty-four energy periods (solar fortnights), each fifteen degrees of the 360-degree sun cycle. We often read that this was established so that farmers could be advised when to plant their crops. In fact, it marks the changes in climate and highlights high-energy days, which were often used for festivals (*see table opposite*). It is possible to offer advice on the types of activities to undertake in each energy period, but the dates for planting crops have to be more specific than this in order to benefit from cosmic and earth energies. The Chinese lunar calendar allows for this, and allows us to link the ancient knowledge with moon-planting knowledge in the West.

THE LUNAR CALENDAR

Ever since hunter-gatherers thousands of years BC carved notches on mammoth bones, human beings have followed the phases of the moon very closely. It was the only means of timekeeping in ancient times and, because ancient peoples worked closely with the natural world, they were able to experience the effects of the changing phases of the moon in all aspects of their lives. This is well documented in many cultures, particularly by the Romans, who left us very detailed agricultural information. On the following pages we will investigate how the moon can improve our gardening practices.

Each Chinese month begins with a new moon. The Chinese lunar calendar is the oldest chronological record in history, dating from the fiftieth year of the reign of the Yellow Emperor. The Chinese almanac, the T'ung Shu, is available in Chinese communities worldwide and contains

information on auspicious times for performing almost any task, including washing hair. It requires complex calculations and is not as yet available in translation. Copies are rare, since it is regarded as a talisman and taken to the temple to be ritually burnt by the priest every year. Martin Palmer translated parts of the Hong Kong version in 1986, and stated that the agricultural information had been removed in 1985 through lack of interest. Professor J. T. Liu has kindly translated some of the planting information from the 1983 edition, and this is shown in the box below (Auspicious Planting Days). The fact that the days are so specifically calculated underlines the importance of the time factor in planting techniques.

We may never know if peasant farmers had access to the information produced by the sages working at the Imperial Court in ancient times. We do know, however, that some farmers today use the annual almanac, the T'ung Shu, to determine the times to plant individual crops. In cultures throughout the world, people have long used observations of the moon and its position in the heavens to decide these times for themselves. The following information will enable gardeners to use this ancient wisdom to grow their plants in accordance with the laws of nature.

THE TWENTY-FOUR SOLAR FORTNIGHTS

SOLAR FORTNIGHT	HIGH-ENERGY DAYS
Spring begins	4, 5 February
Rain	18, 19 February
Hibernation over	5, 6 March
Spring equinox	20, 21 March
Clear and bright	4, 5 April
Rain for grain	20, 21 April
Summer begins	5, 6 May
Grain in bud	21, 22 May
Grain forms beards	5, 6 June
Summer solstice	21, 22 June
Slight heat	7, 8 July
Great heat	22, 23 July
Autumn begins	7, 8 August
Limited heat	23, 24 August
White dew	7, 8 September
Autumn equinox	23, 24 September
Cold dew	8, 9 October
Frost	23, 24 October
Winter begins	7, 8 November
Slight snow	22, 23 November
Heavy snow	7, 8 December
Winter solstice	21, 22 December
Slight cold	5, 6 January
Severe cold	20, 21 January

Auspicious Planting Days

Auspicious planting days are carefully calculated: each day consists of an Earthly Branch, representing the position of the sun on a given day, and a Heavenly Stem, representing the yin or yang quality of the particular element ruling the day. These are discussed more fully on pages 54–5.

- The right days for planting vegetables are:
  ren xu, wu jin, gen yin, xin mao
- The days for planting melon are:
  jia zi, yi chou, xin si, gen zi, ren yin, yi mao
- The right days for harvesting crops are:
  gen wu, ren shen, quei you, ji mao, xin si, ren wu, quei wei, jia wu, quei mao, jia chen, ji you
- The right days for picking the seeds:
  jia xu, yi hai, ren wu, yi you, ren chen, yi mao

PLANTING BY THE MOON

The relationship of the earth, sun, moon and planets affects all life-forms. As the earth revolves on its axis it faces towards the sun and receives light for some of the time, and faces away in darkness for the rest. Night and day are as important for plants as they are for human beings, with night-time (yin) being the time to recharge the batteries after energy has been used up during the course of the day (yang).

The movement of the sun and planets through the heavens cannot be perceived on earth, and yet we receive their influences. The moon, however, being much closer to the earth, can profoundly influence our planting practices.

THE MOON'S PATH

Since Isaac Newton identified the laws of gravity in the seventeenth century, we have accepted that the moon, on its daily cycle round the earth, exerts a gravitational pull which creates the tides. Our ancestors were also aware of this. Pliny and his contemporaries wrote about it over fifteen hundred years earlier. Lesser known is that the same gravitational pull exerts an influence on all water in the earth, including that contained within soil and within all living things. Research done by the biodynamic movement, particularly in Germany by Maria Thun over the past thirty years, shows the beneficial effects on crops of planting at an appropriate time in the moon's cycle. And scientists from Columbia University are reported to have carried out research measuring earth tides, in which they found that the land rises and falls an average of thirty centimetres (twelve inches) twice each day. Scientists have also measured lunar winds, which move across the earth towards the east in the morning and towards the west in the afternoon, at approximately one-twentieth of a mile per hour.

If we observe the moon over the course of a month we will observe that it follows the pattern shown in the diagram below. There are two stages of the waxing moon, leading up to the full moon, followed by two stages of the waning moon. When the moon is waxing, the gravitational pull on the earth is upward. Moisture in the earth and the sap in plants tend to rise upwards. When the moon is waning the opposite is true. (NOTE: As a lunar month is shorter than a solar month, the Chinese add an 'extra' month to their calendar every two or three years.)

PLANTING IN A WAXING MOON

This is the best time to sow and transplant leafy plants which grow above the ground. Herbs cut in this period are more aromatic, and if Christmas trees are cut in a waxing moon the needles are slower to drop. Fruit intended to be eaten immediately should be harvested at this time. It is not, however, the best time for chopping logs, which tend to smoke more when burnt than those cut in a waning moon. Since the moon also waxes and wanes during the course of a day, the best time to plant is in the morning.

PLANTING IN A WANING MOON

This is the best time to sow and transplant those plants which make their growth beneath the ground, such as tubers and carrots. It is also best for plants which need to establish a firm rooting

THE MOON'S PHASES

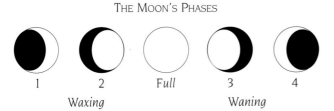

1	2	Full	3	4
Waxing			Waning	

THE MOON'S PHASES		DAYS IN LUNAR MONTH
Waxing	Phase 1	New – 7½
	Phase 2	7½ – 15
Waning	Phase 3	15 – 22½
	Phase 4	22½ – 29

Gardening According to the Moon's Phases

WAXING MOON

• *New Moon* • The complete moon cycle takes approximately 29.6 days. When the moon sits in front of the sun, facing earth, it is the time of the new moon. It is recommended that planting is kept to a minimum for a day or two on either side of the new moon since, should the weather conditions be dry, plants planted at this time will be woody.

• *Phase 1* • This is the best time to sow and plant leaf plants. This phase is particularly suitable for annual plants which produce seeds outside the plant. Examples are the brassica family, including a whole host of vegetables such as cabbage, cauliflower, Brussels sprouts, lettuce and broccoli, as well as cereals.

• *Phase 2* • This is the best time to plant leaf plants which produce seeds inside the plant, such as the legume family. Examples include peas and beans, squashes, aubergines and tomatoes. This is also the time to plant vines.

WANING MOON

• *Full Moon* • Almost fifteen days after the new moon, the moon has travelled round the earth to face the sun and from earth we see the full moon. At the time of the full moon the water in the earth is at its highest and, should weather conditions be damp, then fruit planted at this time will have a tendency to rot. It is therefore recommended that plants should not be planted for a day or two on either side of the full moon.

• *Phase 3* • After the full moon, the moon begins to wane. This is the best time to plant biennials, perennials, bulbs, shrubs and trees, as well as annual root crops. It is also a good time to transplant and take cuttings. Root crops harvested now tend to store longer.

• *Phase 4* • The period coming up to the new moon is when the water has been drawn deep into the earth. It is a barren time and should be used only for weeding, mowing, pruning and other such tasks. Timber may be cut at this time, since the sap will not be rising and the wood will 'bleed' less.

system, like trees and shrubs. Crops and fruit which are to be stored through the winter should be harvested in a waning moon. When planting in a waning moon, the afternoon and early evening are the best times.

MOON PLANTERS OF OLD

A wealth of evidence exists to show that moon-planting techniques were universal. The Romans were prolific writers. Cato's writings (234–149 BC) read like a Feng Shui manual, covering the positioning of buildings, and neighbours and water-courses, as well as planting. He advised on spreading manure 'as the west wind is blowing … at the dark of the moon', on cutting timber 'in the dark of the moon, or in the last phase', and on grafting: 'Figs, olives, apples, pears and vines should be grafted in the dark of the moon, after noon, when the south wind is not blowing.'

Varro (116–27 BC) gave a detailed account of calendars in his agricultural treatise, particularly interesting since he wrote this only eight years after the introduction of the Julian calendar in 45 BC. The Romans used both solar and lunar cycles. The solar advised on types of activities to be carried out, observing eight energetic periods of one-and-a-half months each, rather than the twenty-four used in China. There was also a sixfold division of the seasons, bearing a relationship to the solar and the lunar cycles 'because every product comes to perfection in five stages'. Unfortunately, Varro does not elucidate, but we can now make assumptions as to his meaning.

The Maya had an extremely accurate lunar calendar, and the Islamic and Hebrew years are still based on the lunar calendar, as are those of nomadic tribes across the world. It is thought that Pliny (AD 23–79), in his thirty-seven-volume *Natural History*, obtained his information on moon planting from the Druids, who continue to use the lunar cycle for their celebrations and planting. Some Native American tribes have different names for the moon for every day of the year – Crow Moon, Sap Moon, Warm Moon, for example – to indicate specific energetic times.

Such observations of the moon and the importance of its cycle are evident throughout recorded history. Now we, too, can learn to use these age-old planting techniques to ensure that our gardens are in harmony with the natural energies.

THE CONSTELLATIONS

We have already determined that cosmic chi influences life on earth. Ancient sages identified and named star constellations and planets, and recognized the different influences they have on earth. The diagram below shows earth and the belt of star constellations in the cosmos, in front of which the sun and the planets move. In the West, each constellation has been given a name which we recognize as one of the twelve astrological signs of the zodiac.

THE PRECESSION OF THE EQUINOXES

The astronomy/astrology debate often crops up when discussing moon planting. When the Western calendar was established as we know it, about 4000 years ago, the sun entered the star constellation of Aries on 21 March, the spring equinox. The date was established as zero degrees Aries. In the second century BC, the Greek astronomer Hipparchus discovered that, due to a wobble in the earth's axis of rotation, the sun had been moving away from its original position at the spring equinox. By AD 300, it had moved thirty degrees into the constellation of Pisces. It is now moving into Aquarius. When we follow moon-planting practices, we use the passage of the moon though the constellations as they are now. Strictly speaking, we should use the word 'constellation' and not 'sign', although the latter is far more familiar.

As the moon circles the earth every 27.3 days, it passes through each of the twelve constellations for a period ranging from one-and-a-half to four days. During each period, it activates the particular

qualities of the stars in the constellation, and we feel the force of those influences on earth.

Just as time of birth is important in shaping the types of people we are, the time of sowing and planting is crucial for plants. Most of us achieve good results when using the moon's phases for planting. Others may prefer to be more precise and also use the constellations. In order for us to know the precise times that the moon is changing phase or passing through each constellation, we will either need to be very adept at reading the night sky, or we will need the assistance of a moon chart, a planting guide or a geocentric ephemeris. A selection of those currently available may be found in the Bibliography (*see page* 125).

The forces from the cosmos (cosmic chi), are channelled to earth via the elements. Each constellation is related to one of the four elements perceived in Western culture – Fire, Water, Air and Earth. Each element, and its corresponding constellations or signs, has a beneficial effect on a particular part of the plant as shown in the table above right. The Western planting system is introduced here since it is a comprehensive system already in the public domain. Lunar cycles and cosmic chi are, after all, universal and we will see later how Eastern and Western systems emerge from the same philosophical roots.

Another factor to be taken into consideration is that some signs encourage growth more than others. The most productive signs are the Water signs and the least productive are the Fire signs (*see table right*). Although Cancer, Scorpio and Pisces are the best planting

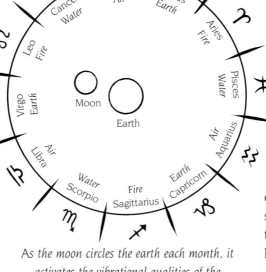

As the moon circles the earth each month, it activates the vibrational qualities of the constellations, which affect all life-forms on earth.

SIGNS, ELEMENTS AND PLANT ORGANS		
Sign	Western Element	Affected Plant Area
Pisces Cancer Scorpio	Water	Leaf
Aries Leo Sagittarius	Fire	Fruit/Seed
Taurus Virgo Capricorn	Earth	Root
Gemini Libra Aquarius	Air	Flower

signs, they are not always suitable for root plants, which may rot in a wet year. The semi-fruitful signs are acceptable for planting when it is not possible to make use of the fruitful days. In addition, some signs are renowned for their special qualities (*see table below right*).

USING THE SIGNS AND ELEMENTS

If we are preparing to plant some lettuce seed, for example, providing the soil and weather conditions are suitable, we would check that the moon was in a waxing phase, preferably the first, and sow the seed in a Water sign – Pisces, Cancer or Scorpio. If our garden is on an exposed windy hillside, we should try to plant in Scorpio for sturdiness. If, on the other hand, we live in a cold valley, we may decide to forgo the Water signs and plant instead in Taurus for hardiness. In a woodland garden, where our aim is to create a drift of bluebells in the spring, or a path flanked by irises, then we should choose to plant the bulbs or rhizomes in the waning moon, in the third phase, and when the moon is passing through the constellation of Libra, which is particularly beneficial for flowers.

To grow a vine on shallow soil, we will choose the moon's second phase – the best for vines – and plant the seed in Pisces, good for root growth, and then transplant in Scorpio, for sturdiness, in phase three, to anchor the roots. In a different location, where wind is not a problem, we might take greater consideration of the fruit, and sow the seeds in Cancer. If one particular plant has produced amazing flowers, we may want to save the seed from that plant. The following year it can be sown in Libra, for beauty, and transplanted in Capricorn in order to have even more seed the following year.

It is obviously not possible to catch the correct phase and sign every time, particularly since the moon only passes through some constellations for two days at a time. The most important considerations, therefore, are to avoid planting in the moon's fourth phase and in a barren sign. The planting tables on pages 118–23 show the best times for planting various plants.

PLANTING AND HEALTH

The use of plants in medicine and their connection to cosmological influences pervades both Eastern and Western tradition. The *Pen Tsao*, around 4000 years old, and the materia medica published by Li Shih-chen in the sixteenth century are still used today. In the sixteenth and seventeenth centuries, Western herbalists such as Gerard and Culpeper were producing similar works, following the earlier research of Dioscorides and Pliny the Elder in the first century AD.

Although the Eastern and Western systems cannot be compared, the theory behind them is strikingly similar. Both recognize planetary influences on parts of the human body, and both use particular plants governed by and related to the various virtues ascribed to the heavenly bodies to cure elemental imbalances.

SIGNS AND THEIR PROPERTIES		
PROPERTY	ATTRIBUTE	SIGN
Growth	Fruitful	Cancer Scorpio Pisces
	Semi-fruitful	Libra Capricorn Taurus
	Barren	Aries Leo Sagittarius Gemini Aquarius Virgo
Special	Abundant crop	Cancer Pisces Virgo (flowers)
	Succulence	Cancer
	Good root growth	Pisces
	Good seed quality	Capricorn
	Beautiful flowers	Libra
	Hardiness	Taurus
	Sturdiness	Scorpio
	Harvesting	Aries Leo Sagittarius Gemini Aquarius

THE PLANETS

Maria Thun's diagram linking each plant organ with a part of the body, based on the work of Rudolf Steiner.

In the previous section, we discovered that each zodiac sign is associated with one of the four (Western) elements and that, in turn, each element is associated with a different plant organ; earlier, we saw that each of the five elements is associated with a part of the body and a particular planet, among other things (*see page 25*). Like their Chinese counterparts, the great Western herbalist astronomers also felt that the planets had a part to play in their association with particular parts of the body and the herbs used to treat them. It was felt that the plant took on the characteristics assigned to its ruling planet and often resembled the part of the body it was to treat (such as yellow flowers for jaundice and liver disorders, and walnuts for strengthening the brain). This became known as the Doctrine of Signatures, and these methods are still used in native cultures worldwide.

diagram also shows the conjunctions of Venus and the sun in the twentieth century in relation to the constellations. Rudolf Steiner, who founded the biodynamic agriculture movement, saw the human being as very much linked to the plant, inasmuch as each plant organ has a direct correspondence with a part of the body: root/head; seed and leaf/arms; and flower and fruit/legs. Furthermore, the proportions of the human body are marked by the planets and each body part is ruled by a zodiac sign. When the signs are joined, they, too, create a pentagram. Pentagram patterns exist in other cultures: it is used in pagan rites as a salutation to the Great Ones, and was also a sign of the Goddess and a talisman in ancient Greece.

By studying the ancient philosophies from any culture we arrive at the same basic beliefs: human beings and all living things on earth are inextricably linked with the forces emanating from the cosmos. Further evidence can be seen if we compare the patterns of the paths of the planets over time and the patterns in the natural world.

THE COSMOS AND NATURE

If we join up the planets on the above diagram, a five-sided figure reminiscent of the five-element cycle is created. We can also see how, in ancient times, human beings were perceived to fit into the cosmological picture: the shape of the pentagram echoes the shape formed by Leonardo da Vinci's illustration of man and his proportions (*see pages* 13 *and* 19). The

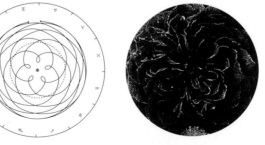

ABOVE. *The pattern produced by the eight-year Venus cycle is mirrored in the arrangement of petals in this rose. The same pattern can be seen in the seeds on a sunflower head.*

RIGHT. *This agricultural calendar from the* Book of Hours *by the Duc de Berry,* AD 1416, *shows summer activities – the crops being harvested in a barren sign, presumably, so the grain will be dry, and the sheep sheared in a waning moon so they will not bleed profusely if cut.*

The Right Place: Plants

'The right place, at the right time' is the
underlying tenet of Feng Shui. It is as true
for plants as it is for people. Plants will
thrive in some places and not in others.
The reason is not always obvious.

One of the first things a Feng Shui practitioner investigates are the neighbours. If there is a problem which has no obvious cause, then the chances are that the answer lies close by. This is especially relevant in the garden. After all, we can move away from noisy or messy neighbours, but plants can only make us aware of their distress if we can read the signs. They thrive if we create the ideal environment in the first place by becoming familiar with plant characteristics and the ecosystems within our garden.

READING THE SIGNS

Visual clues are a useful starting point. We have looked at planting tall and short plants together, and broad- and fine-leaved varieties, in order to create a balanced effect. The rose is a universal favourite, but we – in seeking to improve upon nature – have hybridized it to the point that it is weak, forever sick and requiring treatment. Its antidote is its opposite: something old and stable and pungent. Garlic is the perfect companion for the rose. Most herbs are aromatic due to the large surface area of their fine leaves; some are pleasant, but if we find the smell of rue and wormwood unpleasant, then the chances are that other plants will as well. They are useful as pest repellents in the vegetable garden – but in moderation, or they will repel the vegetables, too. Only by working *with* the plants will we come to understand their natures and their needs.

Ancient peoples were familiar with the signs. They knew when to plant and they also knew what to plant where. Fan Sheng Ching's agricultural manual was full of advice, and Roman writers Cato,

Varro, Pliny and others were knowledgeable in the art of companion planting. A glance around the neighbourhood will tell us which plants will thrive in our gardens. If lilac is much in evidence and we insist on planting azaleas, for example, we are beginning a battle which we will surely lose, since the soil conditions are totally different and no amount of cosseting will make the conditions right.

Insects are integral to an ecosystem. They provide food for birds and other insects, and in turn may prey on others. We can achieve a balance by growing a variety of plants. In a treatise dating back to AD 304, Hsi Han advocated selling oranges together with an ants' nest. Over a thousand years later, Kuang in the *Tung Hsin* wrote '… horticulturists say that in order to grow flowers one must first rear ants'!

WEEDS

Native peoples are in tune with their surroundings. Rainforest dwellers are providing us with useful information on the use of certain plants for healing purposes. Our immediate ancestors also knew how to use plants for healing. Using the Doctrine of Signatures, herbalists like Culpeper and Gerard could tell by the nature of a plant what its habits and likely benefits would be. We, too, could begin to rediscover this information, if we take the time to hear what our gardens are saying to us.

'Weeds are plants in the wrong place.' This well-known phrase relates to the tightly controlled environments of our gardens. Yet in the natural world there are no 'wrong' places. Weeds are amazingly good at offering advice on local conditions and indicating our mistakes. Sorrels, docks and horsetail are acid soil indicators, for example, while foxgloves suggest an absence of lime.

Weeds are not 'bad'. If we are unhappy with them in the garden then we should provide conditions that will discourage them. Some weeds are positively beneficial. Nettles can aid other plants in a number of ways – by increasing disease resistance, by increasing the oils in peppermint and by delaying the rotting process in potatoes and tomatoes. We are all aware of the soothing effect of dock leaves on nettle stings, and the two plants are always found together – an ideal example of companion plants. Another ever-present weed, the dandelion, transports minerals via its long tap root for the benefit of surface-rooting plants, and also improves the humus in the soil, since earthworms are attracted to them.

'REAP WHAT YE SHALL SOW'

Since the garden is a controlled environment, a conscious decision to allow beneficial weeds into our gardens would make *us* the problem neighbours. Yet some plants we do introduce can have far more devastating effects than a few nettles or dandelions. The most persistent weeds are those that we introduce from foreign countries. Sycamore trees, for example, introduced in England in the sixteenth century from Europe and Eastern Asia, have become the scourge of the suburbs. The seedlings grow at an alarming rate, and are soon home to crows and magpies which drive out the small songbirds that we rely on to help us with the garden pests. We then resort to pesticides, and this sets up a system whereby human beings take control of nature, rather than living in harmony with it.

Among the plants on display in garden centres are some of the most persistent weeds, cunningly bred in variegated or dwarf form. Once established in the garden, they can easily revert to their natural state. The worst, Japanese knotweed, originally imported as an ornamental shrub, is so pernicious that it is an offence to plant it in the wild in the UK without a licence. Yet it is sold as *Persicaria virginiana*

– 'painter's palette' – and the unwary are creating themselves a lifetime's problem, since its vast tap roots make it virtually indestructible. Similarly, few have forgiven the Romans for introducing ground elder, yet it is easily available in garden centres as *Aegopodium podagraria* 'Variegatum'.

The Feng Shui gardener asks 'Is it natural?' – that is, would it occur in the natural world without our help. If the answer is 'No', we should seriously reflect on the potential consequences of our actions.

ABOVE. *Sold as* Aegopodium podagraria *'Variegatum', this variegated form of ground elder, once established, can revert to its common form, the scourge of Western gardens.*

ABOVE. Persicaria virginiana, *or 'painter's palette' – plant it if you dare! An offence if planted in the wild in the UK: if it reverts to its common form, a lifetime can be spent trying to eradicate it.*

COMPANION PLANTS

The best way to learn about companion planting is to learn from the greatest of all teachers – the natural world. If we take time to walk in the countryside and sit, watch and listen, we can learn more than any book can teach us. In our gardens we should listen to what nature is trying to communicate to us in order to achieve a balanced and harmonious environment.

MUTUAL SUPPORT

The first thing we notice in the natural world is that there is no bare soil. Where it exists, plants colonize it very quickly and thrive in the positions which are suitable for them. Left to its own devices, large sections of the earth would very quickly revert to forest and swamp and, in the clearings, ground-cover plants interspersed with annuals would be sheltered by perennials, which in turn would be sheltered by shrubs, taller shrubs and finally trees, forming a forest canopy sheltering woodland plants and tree climbers. In the controlled environment of the garden, we could mirror the natural style of planting in which plants of different proportions and growth patterns exist in mutually supportive systems.

Some plants can be used to support others. A useful example of this is the Native American practice known as the Three Sisters: corn acts as a support for beans to climb, and squashes grown underneath provide welcome shade and suppress weeds at the same time. Similarly, hedges can protect other plants by filtering the wind, and tall plants and shrubs provide shade for plants growing beneath.

We can never cease to be amazed at the network of relationships in the natural world. So sensitively are they linked that the removal of one species of plant or insect from an area can have a knock-on effect down the food-chain of which we may be completely unaware. Certain plants, for example, are able to emit a chemical which attracts wasps when they sense aphids feeding from their leaves. The wasps lay their eggs in the aphids, and the aphids, in turn, send out pheromones – airborne chemical signals – to warn off other aphids. Insects are attracted to plants by sight and smell. Some plants reflect ultraviolet light for this purpose. The flowers of marjoram, for example, act in this way to attract bees and moths. Plants may be planted specifically to attract bees, wasps, hover-flies and ladybirds, all of which are necessary for their roles in pollination and in preying on insect pests.

NATURAL CONTROL

If we are familiar with our plants and the ecosystems that exist in our gardens and in neighbouring gardens, we need not use artificial means of dealing with 'pests'. It is rare to find colonies of any one pest in the natural world, since the plants and insects regulate themselves. When we interfere, we upset the balance. If we insist on planting varieties which all attract the same insect pests in the same bed, we

Low planting beneath this clematis shades the roots and gives it the cool root-run it desires. In turn, the graduated planting allows the flowers maximum light.

are asking for trouble. If we introduce plants that we know act as a deterrent to certain pests, or because they attract the predators of certain pests, then we will create a more balanced environment.

Some plants emit root secretions which can prevent diseases in others. Formic acid in the roots of nettles, for example, helps to prevent rot in tomatoes. The legume family, which includes peas and beans, 'fix' nitrogen from the air in their roots with the help of soil bacteria, to make it available to other plants. Strong-smelling plants can mask the smell of other plants and protect them from attack. Onions and carrots grown together confuse each other's main pests. Marigolds in the vegetable garden deter aphids from runner beans. Plants may be used in a sacrificial way to lure pests away from more precious ones: nasturtiums, for example, are often planted to lure blackfly away from beans. The roots of large plants break through heavy soils, preparing the way for the finer roots of other plants. Long- and short-rooted plants grow well together since they are not competing for food.

There are also plants that secrete chemical substances which act as a repellent to other plants attempting to invade their space. Tomatoes, for example, give off root secretions which inhibit the growth of apricot trees, and walnut trees, as documented by Varro in 200 BC, make the soil around them sterile. Wormwood emits toxic root secretions as well as a chemical from its leaves which is washed into the soil when it rains. Few plants will grow near it, yet it is useful in the garden as it deters flea beetles and

Marigolds and runner beans together: a familiar sight in the organic garden. The marigolds help keep the aphids away. Nasturtiums are used for the same purpose.

protects cabbages from caterpillars. Fennel is particularly susceptible to wormwood, while fennel itself inhibits the growth of dwarf beans, tomatoes and kohlrabi. Dill should never be planted near fennel since it picks up its flavour and loses its own. Dill, in turn, benefits a corn crop, but can greatly inhibit carrots. For full details of companion plants, refer to the planting tables on pages 118–23.

THE PFEIFFER METHOD OF SENSITIVE CRYSTALLIZATION

Between 1927 and 1938, Dr Ehrenfried Pfeiffer experimented with copper chloride solution and the sap of plants. The solution was heated and, after the evaporation process, a crystallized fractal pattern was left, unique to each plant species. In experiments on the relationships of plants, the sap of two different varieties was mixed. In the experiment using cucumber and beans the patterns were harmonious, with the cucumber slightly more dominant, showing that the beans were having a beneficial effect on it. Further experiments showed that kohlrabi and tomatoes do not get on well, but that beans benefit turnips.

Later experiments by botanist George Benner showed that saliva also has a unique pattern, and in people who are ill it very much resembles the pattern of the herb that could be used to treat the condition. It would seem that the body seeks a certain vibrational energy to cure itself – a modern-day version of the Doctrine of Signatures, then, and further evidence that all living things have their part to play in the whole universal picture.

Feng Shui in Practice

Feng Shui is the art of placing ourselves in alignment with the beneficial energies emanating from the earth and the cosmos. Intangible forces are difficult to accept and explain, but we can harness them for our benefit to improve the quality of our lives.

Through time, different 'schools' of Feng Shui have evolved. Purists stick rigidly to ancient Chinese texts. Over the centuries, folklore and superstition have become attached, from China and further afield. Recently, the Western mechanistic mind has begun to rationalize the subject, creating easy aids for others to access information. Feng Shui gadgets are appearing, as well as the inevitable do-it-yourself guides. In all this we lose sight of its origins and tamper with unseen energies without fully understanding. If we return to the first principles on our journey, we will begin to unravel the mysteries of this great philosophy. The journey will be long, perhaps over many years; understanding does not come packaged. Other people can only leave clues. It is for us to find them.

THE LANDFORM SCHOOL

The Landform or Form School of Feng Shui is the oldest, and originated in a mountainous area in the south of China. When selecting land and the site for a house, wealthy citizens would employ the services of a shaman or geomancer to investigate the energies around the selected site and advise on the best position in which to build the house. Aligning with the beneficial energies of the universe would ensure good health and wealth for the owner and his family. When the owner died, the family would go through the same process in selecting an auspicious site for the grave, since the well-being of the ancestors is believed to affect the family.

Mountains and water, and the quality of the energies which surround them, play a large part in Form School Feng Shui. Callum Coats in his book *Living Energies*, in describing Viktor Schauberger's (1885–1958) work with natural energies, determines scientifically the ancient geomantic theories. Why, for instance, should water flow from east to west and crops from north to south? How do the shapes of watercourses and terrain affect temperature and soil? It is all here – albeit somewhat less poetically.

The four animals – Tortoise, Dragon, Tiger and Phoenix – provide the ideal setting for a house, offering protection, stability and security.

ASSESSING A SITE
~ *Mountains* ~

Ancient classic texts are illustrated with many different mountain shapes, all of which are given names and generate either a beneficial or a detrimental effect on a site. Mountains can take on the shape of the five elements, but also are identified in animal shapes. Of these, the Dragon, Tiger, Tortoise and Phoenix have particular significance. These animals were thought to possess special properties, and the ideal house would be situated facing toward the south, surrounded by these four animals.

The Black Tortoise to the north is seen as a protector and, along with the White Tiger and Green Dragon on either side, hugs the house and gives it stability. This 'armchair' formation acted as protection from cold northerly winds. In the modern world, in rural areas a hill or a large tree to the rear will serve as the Tortoise, and in cities a fence or a building will suffice.

The Dragon, on the right as you face the house, and the Tiger, on the left, should be balanced. The Dragon may be a hill, with grass and trees, and the Tiger should be a rocky hill. In a town, trees will serve as the Dragon, while the Tiger might be represented by a stone-coloured building. Traditionally the Red Phoenix, to the front, would have been a range of hills in the distance, but today a low brick wall or a rockery will serve. Ideally, if all four creatures can be identified in some way, then the site is an auspicious one.

Dragon's Veins

These are channels of earth energy. They were said to carry the Dragon's blood, and they run from the mountains on to a site. The more veins running to a site, the greater the accumulation of energy there. Activities such as quarrying and tunnelling are thought to damage a Dragon's veins and bring bad fortune. Artificial structures like transmitters can also affect the landscape.

Water

The Water Dragon Classic, an ancient text, is devoted to watercourses. The assessment of the quality of the water can be made by determining the elemental shapes of the patterns rippling on the surface, determined by the wind flow, the speed and direction of the flow and the shape of the pond or lake and its colour. Moving water is dynamic, and yang. Still water is deep and embracing, and yin. Water that meanders slowly through

a site is said to be auspicious, as is a pool in front of the house, known also as a *Ming Tang* (a term used generally to describe open, welcoming space in front of a house). Traditionally, water flowing gently downhill prevented flooding, and where it accumulated in front of a property it was beneficial for crops. Water should also be clean, since stagnant water can cause ill health. Water that moves too fast hurries away the chi. Today, roads and pathways are also considered to be transporters of chi. The appearance of mountains and the shapes of the watercourses are determined to be important, but there are also other factors which need to be taken into consideration when placing plants – or ourselves – in the garden.

Straight Lines

Straight lines do not occur naturally and carry chi too fast. Fences, clothes lines, overhead wires and flat-topped structures may all have this effect or may, in certain instances, give the impression of cutting or slicing (*see also page* 35). Straight roads or paths coming towards a house or a garden seat can feel uncomfortable, and plants do not thrive in these conditions either. Water flowing straight towards a house or a seat is not recommended, but nor should it flow straight away – it is said that this carries wealth away with it. If we consider that wealth is an accumulation of energy, we can see that wildlife colonizes and thrives on the banks of a gently flowing, meandering river, whereas it does not on the banks of fast-moving water. The rushing sound of fast-moving water is not restful, whereas a gentle gurgling or splashing sound is soothing.

Points

The edges of buildings, points of roofs, corners of pergolas, jagged rocks, pointing tree branches and poorly positioned spiked plants can all feel uncomfortable for those in their path. They channel fast-moving chi towards us, producing a knife-like effect in our direction. Also, if you are sitting in the path of the prevailing wind, beware of the arrow on the weather-vane if there is one in your garden.

THE COMPASS SCHOLAR

The Compass School evolved later than the Form School, in an area of China where the landscape is flat. With no natural phenomena to give guidance, geomancers used the heavenly bodies to determine auspicious directions. Pivotal to these calculations was the position of Polaris, the Pole Star, and the Big Dipper, or Great Bear, constellation. The diagram below shows how the Big Dipper (centre) moves through the seasons and energy changes of the year.

A Luo Pan, or Geomancer's Compass, identifies the position of all the identified energy points and may be likened to a computer. A full compass has thirty-five rings, but more commonly they contain between ten and twenty. Within these rings lies information on the structure of the universe, and we use them to position ourselves so that we harness the energies of as many of the auspicious directions as possible. To be entirely accurate for time calculations, a Luo Pan should be divided into 365¼ divisions to mark the sun's route. Ancient compasses were adjusted regularly to take this into account.

Chinese astrologers identified twenty-eight constellations which, when divided into groups of seven, became the Green Dragon, White Tiger, Black

The rings on this Luo Pan diagram contain information that you should by now be familiar with (see opposite for more on the Heavenly Stems and Earthly Branches). Additional information, which would not appear on an authentic Luo Pan, has been added here to show how the different elements connect.

Western astrological signs (*see pages 44–5*).

Bagua and Lo Shu numbers (*see pages 20–21*).

Twelve Earthly Branches representing the twelve months of the lunar year in the Chinese calendar (*see pages 40–1*).

Former Heaven ring showing a static world (*see pages 16–17*).

Later Heaven ring showing the dynamic world (*see pages 16–17*).

Ten Heavenly Stems representing the yin and yang qualities of each of the five elements. The two Earth stems (numbers 5 and 6) do not appear on the Luo Pan since they represent the centre (*see pages 24–5*).

Twenty-four solar fortnights (*see pages 40–1*). If we look at the very simplified version of the compass in the diagram we can begin to see the intricate relationships between the lunar and solar calendars.

Five elements (*see pages 24–5*).

Lunar months shown as the Chinese astrological animals.

The twelve Chinese 'Hours' (double hours) of the day.

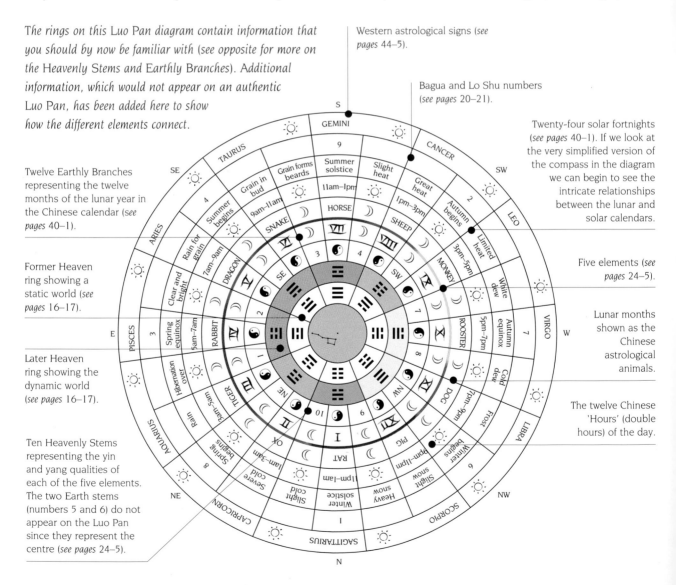

Tortoise and Red Phoenix. Collectively known as the twenty-eight Lunar Mansions and, used in conjunction with the 365¼ divisions (or Chinese degrees) of the compass, they enabled ancient astronomers to predict eclipses and locate the exact position of the sun in relation to the moon. These two rings do not appear on our Luo Pan diagram, which contains only the theory already covered in this book. The sun, moon and Tai Chi symbols have been added to illustrate the interaction of the solar and lunar cycles, and the ring containing the Western zodiac signs shows how Western and Eastern systems are related. The hexagrams of the I Ching also form a ring on the Luo Pan (*see pages 18–19*).

THE FLYING STAR SCHOOL

A ring which is not shown on our diagram is the Twenty-four Directions ring. This describes energy in terms of natural phenomena, such as mountains and water. It includes information on where the energy enters an environment and the qualities of the energy in each of the directions. Each of the eight compass directions is divided into three to make up the twenty-four Flying Stars.

The system of Flying Stars used by some Feng Shui practitioners relates

to house interiors and therefore will not be covered here. It is worth mentioning, however, that it uses the nine positions, or Palaces, of the Later Heaven sequence and the Twenty-four Directions, along with the house age and directions to determine auspicious and inauspicious areas within the house in different time periods.

~ Time and Feng Shui ~

Direction and time are important in the Compass School. Feng Shui calculations are based on the complex interaction of the solar and lunar calendars. In China, time is regarded as cyclical, not linear, as it is perceived in the West. It is divided into periods of twenty, sixty and 180-year cycles. The divisions of the current 180-year cycle are shown in the table below left; the pattern repeats continually, with the next 180-year cycle beginning in 2044.

The year in which a house is built takes its number from the cycle. It is this number which is used in the Flying Star School. If we look at the compass diagram (*far left*), we can see how each sixty-year cycle is made up using the Twelve Earthly Branches and the Ten Heavenly Stems. We can imagine rotating the Heavenly Stems ring. Each of the Heavenly Stems connects with each of the Earthly Branches once every sixty years. This sixty-year cycle is the basis of all the divinational arts in China, including the system of animal horoscopes. By using information from the compass we can position ourselves within the universe to achieve health, wealth and happiness.

ABOVE. *A Feng Shui master and his assistants assess a site using a Luo Pan and measuring rods. One seems to be checking the quality and flow of the water.*

ERA	CYCLE	YEARS
Upper	1	1864–1883
	2	1884–1903
	3	1904–1923
Middle	4	1924–1943
	5	1944–1963
	6	1964–1983
Lower	7	1984–2003
	8	2004–2023
	9	2024–2043

THE INTUITIVE SCHOOL

Some people are more sensitive than others to the 'feel' of a place or situation, or another person. When we begin to work with chi and delve deeper into the philosophy behind Feng Shui, we can all learn the rules. In time, after several years of study, we will feel able to use a compass accurately and chart the energies. Having done this for a while, we will begin to see patterns and pick up signs, and we will probably be able to predict outcomes. We will be competent practitioners. Some of us, however, will instinctively sense the patterns.

Geomancers of old could read the signs in the environment by observing the patterns. Patterns on the water would indicate the type of energies present, and patterns in rocks would indicate local weather conditions. By 'walking the Dragon' – walking through an environment – they could pick up chi 'hot spots': places where chi accumulates and living things thrive. If we lived as hunter-gatherers, our instincts and intuition would be well developed, since we would need them for survival. Feng Shui can effectively enable us to regain these lost arts to improve our lives.

THE BLACK HAT SECT

Black Hat Sect Feng Shui has its roots in Tibet, in Tantric Buddhism. It incorporates a number of elements from Tibet, India and China, and uses Taoist philosophy along with intuition and mysticism to produce Feng Shui enhancements. It is possible to see what lies behind some of these enhancements, and we will come to these on pages 94–5. Others are, according to Professor Lin Yun, *chu-shr* – 'outside our experience'.

THE BAGUA

The Bagua is a modern invention that makes the energies of the Later Heaven sequence – that is, the world we live in – accessible to us all. The increasing popularity of Feng Shui over the past few years is largely due to the fact that, in the Bagua, we have something to relate to and something we can see and use. It is, however, a fraction of the story, but it does give us some useful information which enables us to connect with the energies of our homes and gardens, and also allows us to see how we relate to the energies of time.

THE BAGUA AND TIME

Energy also moves through time. If we look on page 55 we will see that until the year 2003 we are in a 7 cycle. The Bagua

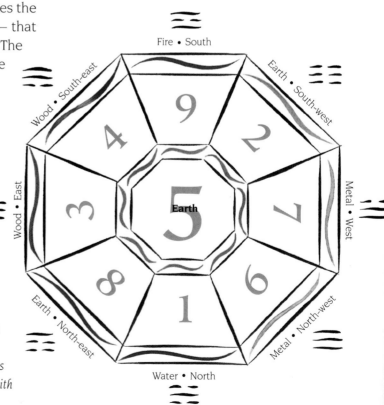

RIGHT. *The Bagua enables us to connect with the energies of the universe; the directions are shown here, together with their respective elements, colours and trigrams.*

diagram shows us that 7 belongs to the Metal element, and its direction is west. To enhance our fortunes until 2003, we can place a metal object in the garden in the western area. This could be a metal sculpture or urn, or even a metal seat. From 2004 onwards we will be in an 8 cycle, and an Earth symbol – terracotta or stone pots, or a special rock – in the north-east would be appropriate.

— Water —

Water accumulates chi for the benefit of the inhabitants of a place. The information in the box below represents a powerful formula for harnessing chi, based on the compass directions of the Bagua and the movement of the Lo Shu numbers through the directions over time. The time periods are related to the movement of the number 5. The number of each cycle sits in the centre of each Bagua, and the other numbers take up positions round it as shown. By placing a suitable water feature in the direction corresponding to the time period, we can harness the beneficial chi from the universe.

THE BAGUA AND DIRECTION

Earlier we saw that the numbers in the Bagua relate to the Lo Shu, and represent life's journey in an energetic pattern. The Bagua shown here reminds us of the relationship between the Lo Shu numbers and the trigrams of the Later Heaven sequence. It also shows the relationship between the Bagua and the five elements. When we lay the template of the Bagua over our home, garden or desk, the energies of each area can be interpreted in relation to the meaning of the corresponding trigram and element.

Using the colours and shapes of the five elements, therefore, it is possible to adjust the energies in a particular area using the Bagua as a guide.

As mentioned on page 38, since the Chinese face south in order to observe the heavenly bodies, south is always positioned at the top and north at the bottom, with east and west correspondingly reversed. Although based on compass directions, the Bagua can assist in Form School assessment of the garden. When it is placed over a garden, south can be regarded as the place in front of us, north as the place behind. To avoid confusion, we can refer to directions by their Form School animal names of Tortoise, Dragon, Tiger and Phoenix – in other words, back, right, left and front respectively as you face the house, and back, left, right and front as you stand with your back to the front entrance.

THE BAGUA AND US

Today, similar techniques are used by Feng Shui practitioners to read the signs in houses. What we surround ourselves with reveals a great deal about us. The way the energy moves through our environment is an indication of the ease or difficulty with which we move through life. If there are stagnant areas in our homes, the chances are that we will be stuck in some aspect of our lives. If we observe the natural way in the garden and observe the interaction of all the living things within it; if we watch the weather over time and are able to predict the effect it will have on crop growth and insect cycles; if we observe the effects of our actions and learn from them, then we are intuitively 'tuned in' to our environment and our path will be easy.

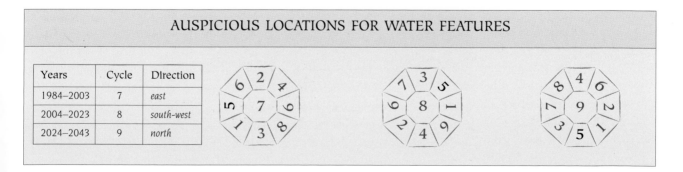

AUSPICIOUS LOCATIONS FOR WATER FEATURES

Years	Cycle	Direction
1984–2003	7	east
2004–2023	8	south-west
2024–2043	9	north

History of Gardens

*For thousands of years gardens have played an
important part in people's lives — as places to
relax, to provide food and medicine, and to
maintain a link with the earth.*

Ever since the hunter-gatherers in prehistoric times gave up their nomadic way of life and settled in one place to grow crops and rear animals, human beings have practised some form of gardening. As early as 3000 BC, rulers in the Near and Far East were creating parks and gardens for sport and pleasure. In China, gardens developed along the same lines. The Han Dynasty in the third century BC was famed for its large formal gardens and parks.

THE PARADISE GARDEN

Persian gardens greatly influenced design throughout the ancient civilized world. In the Islamic world, garden designers used symbolism as well as images from the Koran to create paradise on earth, with gushing fountains and luxuriant planting. As in ancient Chinese culture, cosmology and symbolism also played a central part in Islamic gardens; for example, the importance of the number four, which represents the four seasons, is apparent in garden design.

In Greece, sacred groves on specially selected sites grew up around the temples and public meeting places, and served to provide welcome shade. Planting mirrored the natural world, and flowers were considered to belong to the gods. Following Alexander the Great's campaigns in Persia, more elaborate gardens soon appeared. These were later copied by the Romans, and after the Renaissance became models for many of the great gardens with which we are familiar. Pliny wrote about his own gardens in the first century AD, and was very specific with details of their siting with regard to the sun, the view and cool breezes. He was also concerned about the design of the garden, anxious that it should be linked in a harmonious way with the villa, since he regarded the two as inseparable.

Islamic gardens were full of symbology; note the Bagua shape in the centre of this garden. Despite the formality, several varieties of flowers were planted in each bed — perhaps an early example of companion planting.

THE PHYSIC GARDEN

In the West, from the time of Charlemagne up until the Renaissance, we are mainly aware of the role of the monasteries in creating physic gardens where the monks grew medicinal plants as well as plants for food. Few gardens today are without their herb patch. More than any other aspect of gardening, it is herbs which hold a great fascination for us, almost as if there is some kind of force linking us to the land through them and the particular powers that they possess. Culpeper and Gerard, the great seventeenth-century astrologer

ABOVE. *Physic gardens were our ancestors' pharmacies. This modern version demonstrates that the design has scarcely changed over the centuries.*

BELOW. *The front lawn slopes gently away from this house and trees protect it to the rear. The open space is balanced by the proportions of the house and the planting is minimal.*

herbalists, documented the links between plants, human beings and the cosmos (*see also pages 44–5*).

Renaissance gardens gave way to more natural-looking gardens, albeit with the odd temple here and there, designed by Capability Brown and his contemporaries. We have, however, been discussing the gardens of the wealthy. Most people lived off the land at subsistence level and were therefore very much dependent on the weather and the quality of their environments. As we progressed through the Industrial Revolution to the technological age, gardens became the means for us to cling to our link with the earth. Each country's gardens have their own characteristics, depending on climate and available space. In Britain, for example, where there is a limited amount of land available, gardens are often packed full of plants. In the United States, where much more land is available, planting tends to be far less dense.

A Feng Shui Garden

A Feng Shui garden is one in which the energies
of the earth and cosmos and the cycles of living
things run their natural course. A garden,
therefore, is an 'unnatural' environment.

In Taoism there are two distinct paths. *Tao Jiao* is the religious path and its object is immortality. In order to achieve this state, the external world has to be subdued. The garden expression of this is the Zen garden (*see below*). *Tao Jia* is the philosophical path. Everything in this garden is interlinked and harmonized. In formal Chinese gardens there are few plants and each one has a symbolic significance. They are planted singly so that their individual characteristics are clearly defined. The peach, for example, symbolizes spring and immortality, while bamboo is the symbol of a firm and noble person, who bends in the wind but never breaks. The shape and form of the plants is significant. The flowers are incidental, and single flowers are often meditated upon for their beauty.

Rocks represent mountains or dragons, and their markings represent the veins of chi, or the Dragon veins. There are no lawns, and zigzag paths meander through. Bridges span the water and pavilions appear to float on it.

EAST VERSUS WEST

Oriental outlook differs from the Western view of things. It is responsive to the symbolism of its mythology, superstition and language. This is just as pronounced in Japan as it is in China. In an authentic Tea Garden, a symbolic journey through gates and across stepping stones slows us down on a ritualistic journey, leaving behind the chaos of the external world to find inner peace in the tranquillity of the garden.

RIGHT. *Plants play no part in the Zen garden, which is the ultimate expression of shanshui (or mountain-water), the Chinese term for landscape. The rocks represent the mountains, and the gravel represents the water. The process of raking the gravel and meditating on the fine markings on the rocks is part of the process of understanding the meaning of life on the path to immortality.*

A TRUE FENG SHUI GARDEN

None of the gardens described above are, in fact, Feng Shui gardens. Although each has its own spiritual purpose, the essence of a Feng Shui garden is that it should follow the natural way as far as possible by respecting the landscape and the spirit of the place. Some cultures speak of nature spirits which oversee an environment; others intuitively know how things should be.

If we follow the natural contours of the land and locate the places where chi accumulates, we can create our planting to blend in. Similarly, an awareness of the nature of chi and its movement through a landscape will ensure that our buildings and garden structures also blend in. In following the meandering path of chi, we can create a journey in the garden whereby we simply 'happen' upon things. By observing the energy patterns of the plants, we can ensure that they are located in a beneficial place and planted at times which will aid their natural development cycles. Gardens change over time and can be interesting throughout the day as well as through the seasons. Our aim is to create a tranquil yin space to contrast with the yang world outside – a yin–yang balance on a larger scale – and to gain pleasure from it.

ABOVE. *This Western interpretation of a Japanese garden would never exist in the East. The materials clash and are dull and lifeless, and the dominance of man-made over natural materials is overwhelming. Even the planting is yang. There is little harmony here.*

RIGHT. *This Japanese garden feels timeless. Mossy rocks symbolize longevity and contrast with the energy of the narrow-leaved plants. Water gives the rock in the background a different quality and enlivens the stillness. There is currently a surge of interest in the West in Japanese gardens filled with oriental artefacts. A Feng Shui garden should contain indigenous plants and symbols to respond to the energies of its own culture and landscape.*

THE HEALTHY GARDEN

Described scientifically, soil consists of weathered rock particles and decayed vegetable and animal matter, within which are the various minerals and trace elements required by plants in order for them to grow. While technically correct, this in no way describes the immense importance of soil to all life-forms. Within the soil are millions of micro-organisms, bacteria, fungi, yeasts, all working together to create a medium that will support the plants, which in turn are responsible for most life on earth. Thus the quality of the soil is crucial.

HEALTHY SOIL

Plants have adapted themselves to particular types of soils and climate zones, and the animals and micro-organisms which depend on them (and on each other) have colonized each area. The soil in the area, fed by the remains of the animals and plants over time, builds up all the qualities required to support the living organisms dependent on it. A healthy soil contains humus, which acts as a sponge to retain water. It also contains small creatures, which each have their part to play: for example, earthworms process decaying vegetable matter and woodlice break down wood, which is returned back to the earth. We can often see no use for snails, but if we create a balanced garden they play their part in the ecosystem when they feed the birds and when their shells return to the soil.

When we remove species and introduce alien ones, we move away from the natural order and disrupt the intricate relationships that exist in each area. In order to retain a healthy soil, we have to put back the elements we have removed. The way in which we choose to do this globally will ultimately affect our ability to survive.

– Soil Sickness –

The disappearance of one micro-organism sets up a chain reaction through the support chain, and can have far-reaching implications. Biologists believe that the disappearance of one plant species can lead to the extinction of thirty animal species. Our aim is to take care of the earth and create as natural an environment as possible in our gardens and in the surrounding environment. Few would want to mirror the natural world entirely, but we can use techniques to minimize the damage caused by going against the natural way.

PRESERVING THE SOIL

If we put back into the soil what we remove, then a balance is maintained. If we use artificial fertilizers, we have no way of knowing if we are using too much or too little of each mineral. Artificial chemicals degrade the soil as no humus is being added to conserve moisture and to improve its quality. Soils become dependent on chemicals in a short time, since they have lost their life-giving properties. Many areas have been turned into deserts, as the soil turns to dust and is eroded by the wind.

Soils with no substance become sick, as do the plants which then fall prey to pests. More chemicals are then used, and these destroy not only those pests but also the beneficial organisms in the soil. Pests build up a resistance to the chemicals in time, and consequently more and more chemicals are needed. Chemicals leach from the soil into water supplies and cause major problems, as we have recently begun to experience.

It is modern agricultural practice to plough the fields after the harvest and to fertilize it for the following year's crop, leaving it bare through the winter. In gardens, a similar practice occurs when the summer bedding plants are removed and the vegetable crop used up. John and Helen Philbrick, in *Gardening for Health and Nutrition*, suggest 'uncovered soil is like a wound in the skin of the earth'. On a recent autumn trip to the west of England, famous for its red soil, empty fields on otherwise rolling green hills did indeed resemble open wounds – in Chinese terms, wounded Dragons.

Organic gardeners recommend the use of green manures as a winter crop where no other plants are being grown. They help to improve the structure of the soil by increasing fertility, improving drainage on light soils and breaking up heavy ones to allow air in. Each adds its own special features to an environment. Field beans and lupins are nitrogen fixers. Phacelia and crimson clover attract bees, buckwheat attracts hover-flies, and mustard and winter tares provide a mass of foliage which suppresses weeds. All can be harvested and composted or dug in several weeks before sowing or planting. Chia Ssu-hsieh, in his *Chhi Min Yao Shu*, advised that land should be left fallow only as a last resort, and advocated the use of green and animal manures.

Harvest time on this protected and well-irrigated site. The raised areas prevent the soil from being washed away and the chickens help to keep the crops pest-free while also fertilizing the soil at the same time.

CROP ROTATION				
Year 1	Year 2	Year 3	Year 4	Year 5
LEAF	ROOT	SEED	FLOWER	FRUIT
Cabbage	Carrots	Peas	Jerusalem Artichokes	Strawberries
Spinach	Parsnips	Beans	Flowers	Green Manures
Kale	Beetroot	Tomatoes	Potatoes	
Radishes	Onions	Corn		

In order to maintain a healthy environment in the garden we need to take care of the soil, and to feed it, rather than feeding individual plants. The soil nourishes and nurtures all living things and gives them life.

PREDECESSOR LAW AND CROP ROTATION

Feng Shui practitioners usually ask about the previous occupants of a house, as energetic patterns are transferable. This is also true in the plant world, since continually planting the same plants on the same spot will eventually lead to soil sickness and the plants will not thrive, as their predecessors will have used up the required nutrients. Some plants, particularly the legumes, also return minerals to the soil. Chia Ssu-Hsieh was the first in China to write about crop rotation, suggesting that millet follow mung beans. His ten volumes contain a virtually comprehensive list. Ancient Chinese manuals indicated, for example, that wheat and barley were the best crops for adzuki beans to follow, and that they in turn should precede pumpkins and marrows.

Crop rotation is well known, and was practised for centuries until the introduction of artificial fertilizers. The biodynamic movement recommends a fivefold rotation, which takes into consideration not only the different plant requirements but also incorporates the different energies of the stages of the plant's life cycle – seed, root, leaf, fruit and flower. By accounting for the cosmological energies and the nutritional needs of plants, we can maintain a healthy soil in the natural way.

PERMACULTURE

Permaculture is Form School Feng Shui for the modern age. The word was invented in 1978 by Bill Mollison, an Australian, and is short for permanent agriculture. Permaculture is about resource management and includes energy and water conservation and waste management, local support networks, sustainable systems of food production, and maintaining biodiversity. Many words and phrases from the permaculture movement mirror those used in Feng Shui: for example, the opening sentence of Graham Bell's *The Permaculture Way* reads, 'Permaculture is a way of arranging your life to be happy and abundant.' Permaculturalists observe the natural world in the same way as Feng Shui practitioners. They observe the spiralling nature of energy and weather patterns, and understand the cyclical nature of the universe.

WIND AND WATER

Permaculture manuals give excellent explanations of some of the underlying principles of Feng Shui. Diagrams on siting houses are identical to those in Form School Feng Shui. River diagrams closely match those in the Water Dragon Classic and experienced permaculturalists can tell at which places in a river basin certain types of plants will grow and, by observing the run-off of water in given places, can predict which animals will make their homes there. Thus they, as ancient geomancers of old, are able to work with nature in siting themselves in auspicious positions.

Another feature is energy zones. It is obviously better to place frequently used areas close to the house. Tools in a workshop at the end of the garden are less likely to be used than those close at hand. A herb and salad bed situated close to the house is useful, since few of us would relish a long muddy walk on a cold wet evening. Fruit trees, which are seldom visited, can be positioned further away, and our natural woodland garden can be yet further still. Using permaculture techniques, we plan so that everything in the garden has at least three uses. For example, a hedge can form a wind-break, provide sticks for supporting peas, and nesting sites for birds which prey on plant pests.

The use of spiral beds for planting has been shown to produce greater yields than planting in straight rows, and keyhole beds are the trademark of a permaculture plot, allowing access to all parts of the bed. Companion planting is another feature. Forest gardens are an example of supportive plant networks, where plants mimic their positions in the natural world and vegetables and fruit are interplanted with trees, shrubs and other plants. The emphasis is on perennials rather than annuals, which are time-consuming and labour-intensive.

THE PERMACULTURE DREAM

The permaculture movement recognizes that locally grown food is more nutritious than food which has been transported over long distances. Local support networks are advocated, and many self-supporting groups are being established. The dream is to see city farms producing the food for each area, in order not only to provide more nutritious food but also to cut down on the overuse of agricultural land and the overproduction created by the global economy. The dream actually exists in Shanghai, which supports its vast population in this way.

The loss of biodiversity is a problem which conservationists worldwide are concerned about. The permaculture way of life offers an alternative to the world in which multinational companies control all aspects of the agricultural process, from seed to food production and its transportation. Plants are being genetically engineered to produce pest- and disease-resistant varieties, resulting in loss in biodiversity. EU subsidies, for example, encourage farmers to grow monocultural crops, increasing the degradation of the soil and the potential for disease. The Irish potato famine of 1846, in which half a million people died, showed the folly of relying on a single cash crop. To counteract this trend, seed banks are now being established by conservationists around the world to preserve native species of plant and vegetable seeds.

A LONG-TERM SOLUTION

Permaculture invites us to predict the long-term consequences of actions. Short-term solutions are often more attractive, allowing instant gratification, but often we discount fundamental problems when we opt for the 'quick fix'. If, for example, we have a plot infested with bindweed, we can choose to spray it with chemicals, but the effect on the ecosystem will be devastating. Attempting to dig bindweed is fruitless, since each part of its brittle root will develop into a new plant and make the problem worse. The non-chemical way to eradicate it is to deprive it of light for a year or two. We can plant through black plastic sheeting, allowing for the fact that the bindweed will find any chink of light and use our plants as supports. Microporous sheeting will also block the light, but at least lets the rain through. In both instances, we must be aware of what we are doing to the soil. Plants will eventually die, starved of light, water, air and the beneficial ministrations of soil micro-organisms which will have suffocated under the mulch in the dank and stagnant soil (*see also page 66*). Cardboard and hessian-backed wool carpet, although not attractive, will rot down in a year or two, improving the soil texture and allowing us to plant through them in the meantime.

Like Feng Shui, permaculture offers us a different view of life, cooperating with – rather than dominating – the natural world. It uses the ancient knowledge combined with the functional technology from the modern world to create and manage harmonious environments which respect that all living things are part of a single system.

Herbs and flowers used as companion plants can be planted with crops in these beds.

The meandering shape of a spiral bed mimics the shapes in the natural world and provides a larger planting area than traditional straight lines.

Annual crops planted in these beds will enable crop rotation to take place, thus preventing the soil becoming depleted of some minerals and trace elements.

A herb bed here, which can also be used for fast-growing salad crops, will attract bees and beneficial insects into the vegetable garden.

Graduated planting allows for protection and support of less hardy annual crops.

The keyhole areas allow access to all parts of the bed for maintenance and provide turning points for wheelbarrows.

A paved or gravelled area here, with a seat to allow us to pause and admire the fruits of our labours!

These keyhole beds are a trademark of permaculture design. They follow the meandering course of nature and allow access to all parts of the plot without having to tread on the soil.

ORGANIC GARDENING

Organic gardening movements exist in countries worldwide. One of the leading voices is HRH The Prince of Wales, who gardens and farms organically. At the Lady Eve Balfour memorial lecture, delivered in 1996 in London to mark the fiftieth anniversary of the Soil Association, he highlighted issues of concern to environmentalists and nutritionists worldwide and quoted from Lady Eve: 'The health of soil, plant, animal and man is one and indivisible.'

Organic gardeners try, as far as possible, to be self-sufficient. This means that external influences – such as imported soils, artificial fertilizers and chemicals – are kept to a minimum. If pests become a problem then natural means are used to control them, using plant extracts or, if necessary, non-persistent soap sprays based on fatty acids. A recent innovation has been the introduction of predators, for example parasitic wasps, to control greenhouse pests. This aspect of organic gardening has no place in the Feng Shui garden, since we are tampering with an ecosystem and we can never be sure of the consequences of these actions. The release of genetically engineered organisms into the environment with absolutely no control over their behaviour patterns is perhaps the greatest human folly yet, and is shunned by organic gardeners as well as anyone concerned about the environment.

The principal aim of organic gardeners is to build up a fertile growing medium in a natural way. The 'no-dig' system depends on first manuring the soil, and then creating raised beds which are mulched regularly with compost, which serves to raise the fertility of the soil and reduce weed growth by cutting out the light. In recent years, man-made mulches have been introduced, which again have no place in the Feng Shui garden. The use of black plastic, apart from its lack of aesthetic appeal, prevents the natural elements and cosmic influences from reaching the soil, harbours pests, prevents natural feeding and, over time,

makes the soil sick. The use of bark chippings and sheet mulching with recently cut plant material has also become popular. These processes do not occur naturally, since the soil activity of the micro-organisms and the use of nitrogen for the breakdown process detracts from the plants growing in the soil. We must remember the fundamental criterion: is it natural?

COMPOST AND MANURE

We probably do not notice insect carcasses, but are quick to remove dead birds and animals, to sweep up leaves, to burn prunings and to take weeds to the local rubbish dump. Yet all these are valuable in returning life to the soil. A compost heap is the best way of storing and processing all

Bees and a good soil play their part in the production of these healthy-looking vegetables. Close planting prevents weeds and retains moisture, and companion planting keeps pests at bay.

these materials until they have rotted down into a form in which they may be returned to the soil in order to enrich it. Any naturally occurring, unprocessed product may be included.

By far the most beneficial way of returning nutrients to the soil is in the form of animal manure. Working on the principle of 'what goes in, must come out', we can determine whether the rearing processes of the animals which produce the manure conflict with our ideas on the use of chemicals and unnatural feeding practices.

The micro-organisms working in the soil are known to be most active at the time of the equinoxes – that is, at the times of year when we are clearing the soil, in spring and autumn. These are the times to make compost heaps and to put manure and compost on to the soil, where they can be worked on by the bacteria.

BIODYNAMICS

Biodynamics, from the Greek *bios* – life, and *dynamis* – energy, is a holistic system of organic gardening. It evolved following a series of lectures on agriculture given by Rudolf Steiner in 1924, and much of the theory is in line with Feng Shui philosophy. Principally concerned with soil fertility, companion planting and crop rotation, biodynamics also encompasses phenomenology, cosmology and nutrition.

Some plants are recognized as having special properties, particularly nettle and comfrey, used as liquid feeds and also in compost. Manure and compost play an important role, and their use differs from that in the organic garden by the use of special 'preparations' which activate the soil. Steiner believed that cosmic energies play as fundamental a part in the growth process as water and minerals. Spray preparations are stirred for an hour in a particular way so as to create chaos in the water to harness the vibrational energies from the cosmos. Present-day research into cosmological influences on plants and planting has come from those who studied with Steiner, in particular Maria Thun in Germany (*see Bibliography on page* 125).

Biodynamic gardeners rarely water plants, since inadequate watering encourages plant roots to grow to the soil surface and in hot weather they can be scorched. In using the specially prepared composts to improve the water-holding capacity of the soil and the natural rhythms of the earth and the moon, it is possible to harness the earth's natural moisture and encourage plant roots to grow downwards. This enables them to find moisture lower down in the earth and keeps them cool. The fact that most biodynamic, organic and permaculture growers tend to use the raised-bed, no-dig method of planting ensures that water is conserved in the soil and not allowed to evaporate away.

The Preparations

The preparations are homoeopathic doses of natural plant and mineral extracts which are inserted into the manure or compost heap or diluted and sprayed on to the soil to invest it with special properties.

• *Preparation 500* • This is made from treated cow manure and sprayed directly on to the soil. Its purpose is to promote root activity and stimulate the micro-organisms in the soil. It is used in spring and autumn, and always in the afternoon.

• *Preparation 501* • This is made from ground quartz or silica. Steiner saw silica, present in the earth's crust and in plants like *Equisetum arvense* (horsetail), as a special channel for cosmic forces. It is sprayed after Preparation 500 directly on to the plants when they are fully grown, and is always sprayed in the morning.

• *Preparations 502–507* • These are a set, used together, and a pinch of each one can treat several tons of compost. They are made from yarrow, camomile flowers, stinging nettles, oak bark, dandelion flowers and valerian flowers, and prepared in a special energetic way as described by Steiner. These six preparations are thought to act as channels for cosmic vibrations within the compost or manure heap.

• *Preparation 508* • This is used to combat fungal diseases and is made into a tea from *Equisetum arvense*.

♦ Part Two ♦

CREATING A FENG SHUI GARDEN

With an understanding of Feng Shui
principles, we can instinctively create
a beautiful, harmonious space in our
gardens and, thus, in our lives.

❦

Planning a Feng Shui Garden

We need to consider the wider environment as well as the features within our own garden. In this section, a house and its surrounding plot has been used by way of an example, to demonstrate how to assess an environment and make improvements.

ASSESSING THE ENVIRONMENT

LOCATION

When buying a house we are told that 'location is everything'. The energy of an area is particularly important, and people are naturally attracted to areas with the feel-good factor. Run-down areas are best avoided, but since energy is cyclic over time, phases of regeneration and stagnation do occur. Stagnation may be followed by regeneration, just as ultimately yin changes to yang, and vice versa.

The property should be in balance and harmony with the surrounding environment. If high buildings border the property, they will create shade and wind turbulence. This yang energy will need balancing with the yin energy of trees and plants. Still water balances yang features, and by reflecting an overpowering tree or building can appear literally to 'soak it up'.

Assessing the Location

• Positive features include: healthy vegetation; songbirds; well-kept houses and gardens; fertile soil; trees; fresh air and good air flow; fresh, slow-moving water.

• Negative features include: stagnant or fast-moving water; electrical pylons and overhead cables; electromagnetic wave transmitters; poor air quality caused by gasometers; smoking chimneys; excessive traffic, especially traffic jams; sick-looking vegetation; crows, magpies and pigeons; poorly kept gardens; schools. The latter may seem strange to those unfamiliar with the inherent behaviour patterns of small 'yang' persons who appear unable to restrain themselves from decapitating plants, swinging from branches and disposing of rubbish on their way home from school!

Once we have chosen a location and chosen a property it is advisable to walk around the area. There are a number of positive and negative features to look out for (*see box below left*).

PREDECESSORS

One of the first questions to ask is: Who lived here before? Try to investigate back as far as possible, since previous activities and cultivation methods have implications for our use of the garden. Questions worth asking are:

• What was the land used for? There is a difference between land used as a market garden or cricket pitch, and that which served as a landfill site or paint factory, for instance.

• Has there been extensive decoration or renovation? Discover where the excess concrete was dumped, or where chemicals were disposed of.

• What were the hobbies of the previous owners? If the teenagers of the household owned motorbikes, for example, where did they change the oil or bury old batteries?

• What were the favoured plants? Shrubs and perennials may have been in position for a long time, leaving the soil in need of feeding, or there may be roses and annuals which will almost certainly have been fed, but artificially, and inevitably sprayed with chemicals.

• What is the condition of the grass? Perfect green grass indicates chemical maintenance and watering.

• Were there any pets fouling the garden? Bear this in mind if your young child will be playing in the garden, or if you are planning to grow vegetables.

NEIGHBOURS

Neighbours are extremely important. If they argue, then barriers are created – both social and physical – and we may not welcome high fences or hedges that block our light. If neighbours have obviously used chemical sprays, the fallout spray on to our soil will have implications if we want to grow vegetables organically.

Neighbours' pets can also be a problem. An adored tabby can be a menace in a newly planted border and can destroy whole families of birds in a day. If the neighbours have a swimming pool, this can be a plus point for a family with young children, but a potential nightmare for an author or night worker. The smell of barbecues can have a rather limited appeal for a vegetarian living nearby, and football nets and tennis courts in close proximity to the garden could result in squashed plants and, if you have a pond, surprised goldfish!

DIRECTION
~ Wind ~

Direction is important in terms of who we are and where we position ourselves. The direction the house faces will determine the position of the sun at various times of the day and the direction of the prevailing winds. In ancient China, the ideal position to face was south, since the water channels so necessary for growing and transporting crops would have been located there. In the West, we prefer to face north so that our gardens are south-facing, and this is something which needs consideration in assessing an environment. Being protected from the prevailing winds is important. In the northern hemisphere these are north-easterly, bringing cold dry winds, and south-westerly, bringing moist warm winds. The directions in the southern hemisphere are south-easterly for cold winds, and north-westerly for warm moist winds.

~ Water ~

Where a river runs through a site at the back of a house, we are often told that this is not good in Feng Shui terms. It will, however, often be obvious to a practitioner that this is in fact the mouth of chi. There is nothing 'wrong' in this: it merely means that the energies of the place will need adjusting accordingly. 'Rules', if strictly followed, can often fly in the face of nature. If our front garden slopes upwards, for example, then this is not the place for too much water or for drains, since water flows down.

We should not take a pedantic approach to Feng Shui. We need to 'read' the energies of the place before we can make judgements on it. The energies existing in and around a property are often obvious. Sometimes there are complex systems of energies at work, and it becomes more difficult to interpret the energies within and outside the house. This is why it is impossible to carry out a Feng Shui survey from a plan.

BALANCE

The yin–yang balance is important. The area should neither be waterlogged nor too dry. Marshland areas can be particularly difficult places to live in; such areas in the UK are famed for their insular communities. Living in wet areas can also affect physical health, although dry areas bring their own problems as well – lack of water can have a devastating effect on crop growth and on local vegetation, which plays a major, if unseen, role in the ecosystem.

High mountains can be overpowering, and flat land can be cold and turbulent in winter while being subject to short periods of intense heat in summer. Local features should be appealing to look at. Dead trees and strange-shaped rocks, for example, can affect us. The Chinese classics analyse the shapes of many rock formations and name them according to the effect they are likely to have on those who live in close proximity to them, and environmental damage such as deforestation and quarrying leaves scars on both the landscape and our minds. Using the principles of the Form School, yin and yang and the five elements, we can ensure that we create balance and harmony in our gardens.

WIND AND WATER

Wind and water are terms which cover several factors in Feng Shui apart from the obvious qualities and directions of wind and water. 'Wind' takes into account the movement of wind around buildings and garden structures and through vegetation. However, it also covers the unseen movement of chi through an environment – for example, where vegetation grows well or is stressed – as well as the action of the sun's rays and solar and lunar winds, and the vibrational qualities emanating from the planets and the cosmos. It covers the interaction of plants and our interaction with neighbours.

'Water' affects the way we move through our environment. It covers access to and through the property: road access to schools, workplaces, shops and leisure facilities, the movement of people and cars going past the property, and within the garden, paths and access through beds. Permaculture zones come under 'water'. The example opposite demonstrates the factors which need to be considered.

What to Look For in Your Neighbourhood

- 1 *Three very large sycamores. They will seed everywhere and will be a constant problem.*
- 2 *If neighbours' gardens are not well-maintained, these trees will reach 10 metres (33 feet) or more in a few years, affecting light and nearby plants.*
- 3 *The point of the walls and roof creates sha chi – a 'poison arrow' – towards the back of the house. The tree in front will cover it when it grows taller.*
- 4 *The gap between the houses opposite creates sha chi, since it can form a wind tunnel. The Eastern interpretation is of money running away – after all, alleyways do make good escape routes for burglars!*
- 5 *The lamp-post and sycamore tree, which has branches chopped off regularly leaving stumps pointing at the house, create negative chi.*
- 6 *Plants and weeds in neighbouring gardens indicate soil type. Lilac and viburnum indicate alkaline soil. Azalea lovers will be disappointed. Ground elder grows in alkaline soil, while mare's tail and creeping thistle thrive on acid soils.*
- 7 *Absent neighbours have their advantages and disadvantages. We can helpfully cut their adjoining hedge and thus control the height. We may hate privet, but at least it prevents the dandelion seeds blowing across.*
- 8 *This Leylandii hedge is too far away to create root damage or to block the view. Here it is useful in giving protection against the 'poison arrow' from the roof of the house on the corner.*
- 9 *Communal gardens may prove a problem, since it is difficult to determine responsibility for their upkeep. This no-man's land is planted with snowberry (Symphoricarpus albus), which encroaches and interferes with the garage door.*

Tiger

- 10 *Elder trees can indicate geopathic stress. Stress avoiders, both plants and animals, will have difficulty along the stress line. A dog kennel is not a good idea here, but neighbourhood cats will love sitting on the fence.*
- 11 *The point of the garage roof and the corner of the neighbouring apartment block (number 14) are aimed at the kitchen. Check if remedial action is possible.*
- 12 *A pathway runs behind the house, indicating insecurity there.*
- 13 *Electricity substations and telephone boxes can create unseen vibrations. If these were closer they could be cause for concern.*
- 14 *The windows of the apartments overlook the kitchen. This may prove uncomfortable for both neighbours. Check if screening is possible.*
- 15 *The north-easterly prevailing wind is slowed by the hedge in the next garden.*
- 16 *The south-west wind is a problem, since the corner of the apartment block and the garage create turbulence and strong gusts of wind.*

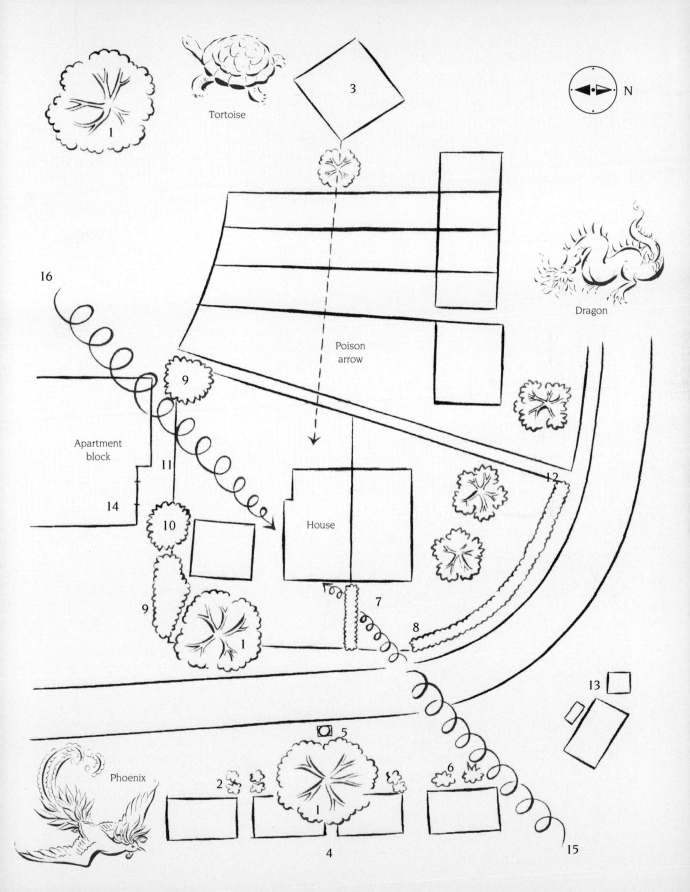

N

Tortoise

3

16

Poison
arrow

Dragon

9

Apartment
block

11

14

10

9

House

1

7

8

12

13

5

Phoenix

2

1

6

4

15

CREATING THE GARDEN PLAN

Before changing anything in our environment, it is advisable simply to observe the garden over time – ideally for a year, to see it through each season. A tree that we have earmarked to shade the terrace in the summer, for example, may prove to be home to squabbling starlings each evening. It is useful to make a note of features and plants we wish to keep, and essential to mark the position of bulbs since we will surely forget their location.

Ease of movement round the garden should be noted, particularly in the summer when a small insignificant shrub can transform into a large floppy nuisance and may need relocating. External features that affect the garden and any features within the garden that make us feel uncomfortable should be noted, along with plants which cause distress to their neighbours and the favoured nesting places of wildlife.

Observing Garden Features

• 1 *This large sycamore tree dominates the garden and affects the neighbours in the apartment block. The ground under it is barren and nothing grows.*

• 2 *This elder tree does not fare well under the sycamore tree.*

• 3 *The roots of this plant from next door are breaking up the paving and the plant is growing through.*

• 4 *Weeds are growing through the broken concrete steps and the paving.*

• 5 *Climbers from next door are strangling the plants in this narrow border and are a constant irritation to those sitting on the garden seat.*

• 6 *The water from the garage roof runs into a land drain and thus waters the plants on the other side of the fence which constantly grow through.*

• 7 *This seat faces the kitchen windows of several apartments in the block opposite. The opening and closing of windows and constant movement within the apartments is not restful.*

• 8 *This quick-growing shrub screens the toilet window. It is tall and narrow, and needs constant pruning to maintain its height and prevent it encroaching on to the path.*

• 9 *This shrub is also an obstacle to reaching the herb garden from the kitchen. The grass path is a nuisance if wet.*

• 10 *The greenhouse creates shade in the vegetable garden and the corner sends a 'poison arrow' towards the seat. The narrow grass paths around it are difficult to mow.*

• 11 *Plants along this fence may show signs of geopathic stress.*

• 12 *The rockery is full of ground elder and weeds.*

• 13 *In order to fit it in, the garage has been built in line with the boundary. The paving follows the line of the garage, not the house, causing a visual dilemma.*

• 14 *Some protection will be necessary at the rear to prevent unwanted access from this public right of way.*

• 15 *The corner of the pond points at the garden table and the house. Because it is so exposed, the water is never clear and the fish are fair game for the local cats. The steep sides do not allow frogs and toads to climb out.*

• 16 *This is not a good choice for a specimen tree (one planted in isolation), since its suckers come up in the grass and beds.*

• 17 *The straight path to the front door channels sha chi.*

• 18 *The crazy paving on the drive and path create a broken-up and unstable entrance to the property.*

• 19 *Only the odd weed grows in this odd-shaped bed. The compacted soil indicates that quantities of water and/or chemical substances have been deposited there.*

• 20 *Frequent digging and pruning are required to prevent these plants taking over this bed.*

• 21 *Since the garden slopes down to the road, this bed is difficult to water as the water runs off.*

• 22 *The trunk of this tree pushes over the fence and the roots raise up the paving. It seeds itself all over the garden.*

• 23 *The hedge in the neighbouring garden will drain all the moisture from this narrow bed. Low-growing plants will have their surface roots scorched by the heat of the path in summer.*

• 24 *The corners on this low wall may graze ankles at night.*

• 25 *The blackbirds nesting in this shrub create cosmetic and health problems on the garden table.*

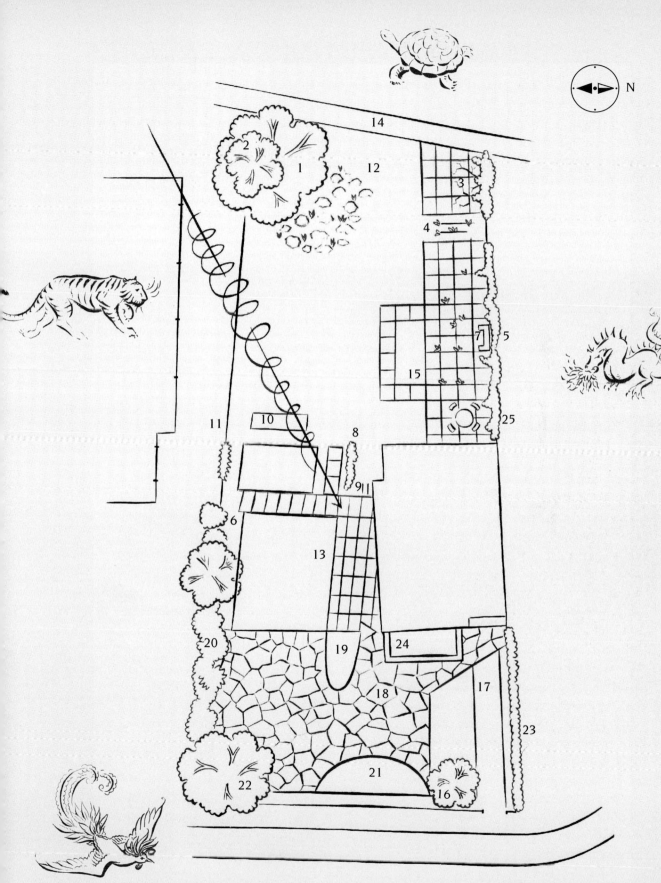

N

WORKING WITH SHAPES

PLOT SHAPES

Symmetry is important in Feng Shui. Where plots are not regular we should try to create the illusion of regularity. In Diagram 1, the boundaries need pushing out; this illusion can be created by careful planting. In Diagram 2, a trellis or planters will square off the missing space, as will a tree or post positioned in the missing corner. If there is no access to the garden, place a mirror or a picture

ABOVE. *Used in a confined space or to make a shape regular, a* trompe l'oeil *can make all the difference.*

with a long-distance view on the wall inside the house. Diagram 3 shows how to divide an irregular shape into two regular ones, or we could push back the shorter wall using a mirror or *trompe l'oeil* (*see above*). In Diagram 4, planting creates regular shapes within an irregular plot.

SLOPES

Where the front garden slopes gently away from the house, a wide view is created and excess water can drain away. Steep slopes create the feeling of a struggle and symbolically represent finances rolling away. A wall, hedge or fence in the Phoenix

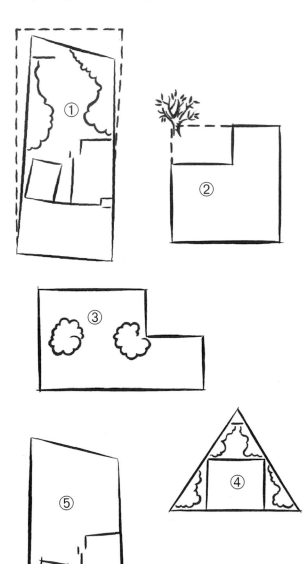

KEY
1. *Pushing out boundaries*
2. *Squaring off missing space*
3. *Dividing irregular shapes*
4. *Dealing with triangles*
5. *Raising the view*

position will help contain the chi. The back garden should be slightly higher than the front, again for drainage purposes. If it slopes away, there is a feeling of instability in the Tortoise position. If the road in front of the house slopes, we may feel off balance and can rectify this by placing something tall – a lamp-post, columnar tree or obelisk, for instance – at the lowest point of the slope to raise the view (*see Diagram* 5).

BOUNDARIES

Protection is the aim of Feng Shui and we should protect our boundaries, particularly where there are public rights of way nearby. Robert Frost's poem *Mending Wall* suggests that 'good fences make good neighbours'. Broken-down fences, with unwanted plants growing through, hedges which require constant trimming, tall trees and shrubs blocking light and using up all the soil moisture, the unmended hole which small yapping dogs fling themselves through … all these unsettle us and affect our peace of mind. Thus, while protection is paramount in Feng Shui, it must also be considered in terms of harmony.

The front fence or hedge is the Phoenix and should be low enough for us to see beyond: waist height or the height of the window sill are useful measures. If hedges and fences at the front of a house are designed to box us in and keep the world out, we may need to question our motives. Ideally the Dragon should be slightly higher than the Tiger; in ancient times this would have protected the perfect south-facing house from the cold north-east winds.

ENTRANCES

Often one entrance serves for both cars and people, and thus we never really leave the office behind; where we enter the house through a door from the garage, we do not have the space to shake off the outside world. Ideally there should be a separate pedestrian entrance and a pleasant interlude between our working life and home life, as in Diagram 6.

PONDS AND POOLS

Ponds and swimming pools should be in proportion to their environment. Water is energizing, but too close to the house it can be overwhelming and detrimental, particularly if our personal element is not in harmony with it. Ponds should follow shapes from the natural world and a large circumference will encourage more wildlife. Diagrams 7 and 8 show the difference in area between the usual rounded pond and a more natural one. Sharp corners are not recommended since they create sha chi if pointing at the house (*see Diagram* 9). Rectangular swimming pools are best if rounded into an oval shape at the ends, and kidney-shaped pools are also acceptable. Bright-blue chlorinated water and the garish colours sometimes found in pool tiles can look harsh in a natural setting. Bear in mind the five elements when designing and siting a pool.

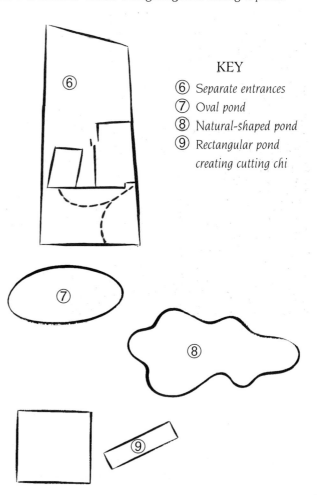

KEY

⑥ *Separate entrances*
⑦ *Oval pond*
⑧ *Natural-shaped pond*
⑨ *Rectangular pond creating cutting chi*

Clearing Clutter

Clutter can be actual physical mess, but can also indicate our state of mind. It is the debris we create in our inner and outer worlds which prevents us moving on. A clutter-free environment can help us mentally to address life's issues.

Clutter is stuck energy. It usually indicates an unfinished task. At best, unfinished tasks are a minor source of irritation; at worst, they can lead to even greater problems and can prevent us from moving on in our lives. Clutter in the garden covers a whole range of aspects, from a pile of unwashed flowerpots to plants that are situated in the wrong place.

DEBRIS
Debris can include those unwashed pots which pile up in corners. It can also include the accumulation of sweet wrappers and fast-food litter if you happen to live near an outlet. Leaves in the autumn, finished annuals and the stems and flower heads of perennial plants should be cleared up and composted once they have served to feed birds with their seeds. If left, they will overwinter pests or, if wet, cause plants underneath them to rot. Hanging baskets and pots of annual plants are best cleared in the autumn, rather than being a constant reminder all winter of something that needs to be done. Better

still, use perennial plants planted with annuals to provide some summer colour, leaving something pleasant to look at in the winter.

PLANTS IN THE WRONG PLACE
It is a good idea to know the growing habits of plants before we plant them. Trees and shrubs planted too near a path or seat will need regular pruning to prevent them from causing an obstruction. If this happens, it is best to move the plant or the seat to prevent this becoming a constant problem. Trees too near a house may interfere with the drains and raise the paving. Plants at ankle level can be a nuisance, and climbing plants and tall perennials that we fail to support can irritate us year after year unless we resolve to take some form of remedial action.

Seedlings of trees like laburnum and sycamore will soon become small trees unless we remove them on sight, and plants like columbine and nigella, which seed readily, will not suit the hour-a-week gardener. Bindweed, which appears to grow

These roses need constant attention and should be moved if the seat is to be used. A less vigorous thornless variety could be planted instead, once the soil has recovered.

several metres every day, and creeping thistles, whose tap roots grow at an alarming rate, are best dealt with straight away rather than in a month's time, when they will have become not one but several plants. If we are at all lawn-proud, it is best that we beat our offspring to those lovely, fluffy dandelion heads, too!

WANDERING PLANTS

A number of plants send out suckers from their roots, and these can be a menace, particularly in a small garden. They appear in borders and break up paving. Lilac, a great favourite for alkaline conditions, has a tendency to do this. One of the worst offenders is the stag's horn sumach, considered a weed in parts of the United States where it has colonized hillsides, but often found as a single specimen tree in Britain. Cherry and plum trees also have this tendency, and two shrubs worth avoiding in a small or well-regulated garden are *Kerria japonica* and *Symphoricarpus albus*, the snowberry.

IRRITANTS

If a path or a patio is cracking up, it is best to repair it immediately, before it gets worse. Crazy paving is not recommended in Feng Shui, since it symbolizes difficulties and instability. Squeaking gates, shed doors which stick, a mouse hole into the fruit store – all of these will take moments to fix but will nag away at us unless we fix them soon. Plants can also be irritating. High-maintenance plants which need endless training and tidying, or

'Blob, blob, blob' is Christopher Lloyd's bored description of the high-maintenance rose garden at Great Dixter, England, which he transformed into this fiery Mediterranean garden requiring less spraying and upkeep.

those which attract vast numbers of sucking and gnawing insects, might better be replaced with less-demanding ones.

WATERING

Annual plants, vegetables in growing bags, pots and tubs all need regular watering to keep them healthy. At the end of a busy day, often the last thing we want to do is spend two hours watering the garden, and, indeed, with current water shortages we should be seriously thinking of ways to conserve water and use it wisely. With careful planning, and the use of leaking hoses, we can eradicate this chore and save water. Little of the water sprayed on to the soil with hosepipes actually benefits the plant. Some will run off and soil penetration is often negligible. It is preferable to surround plants with leaking hoses or to sink plastic bottles into the soil around particularly thirsty individual plants and water directly into them to channel the water to the roots. Mulching after a downpour will prevent moisture loss by evaporation, and good soil maintenance will do much to eradicate the need for watering at all.

A CHANGE FOR THE BETTER

Change is the essence of Feng Shui. Nothing remains the same for ever. Just because an elderly relative planted a certain plant and it was their favourite does not mean it has to be ours as well. If we dislike it, we should remove it and replace it with something to give *us* pleasure.

Creating the Garden

*Having identified the four animals, we need to
investigate and eliminate, if possible, any problems
with our boundaries and the surrounding environment.
We can then think about the other features within the
garden. These aspects are discussed here in reference
to the example used on pages 72–5.*

EXTERNAL FEATURES

TORTOISE

The roof of the house at the rear is pointing at the bedroom windows. The tree in front will soon grow sufficiently to cover it. Meanwhile, window stickers will deal with it in children's rooms. Adults could counteract its effect by draping material over a pelmet or curtain pole.

TIGER

The apartment block is overpowering and a corner of the building shoots a poison arrow at the kitchen. Two kitchen windows are facing each other, which can be uncomfortable for both parties. A fast-growing conifer will quickly grow too tall and outgrow the space. Its roots would interfere with the drains and nothing would grow near it. A slow-grower will take time, but will be worth the wait. Meanwhile, there are other ways to deal with the situation. A reflective metal ball on the window sill will deflect the image and render it less of a problem. Imaginative use of cafe blinds (covering the bottom half of a window) or beads will also help to alleviate the problem. For our health's sake, we should not be tempted to draw the curtains and shut ourselves away, thus blocking out the view of the garden and the sky.

DRAGON

We can identify the Dragon in the house on the bend and the three large trees, none of which present a problem of any kind.

PHOENIX

The large tree and the lamp-post opposite the house create sha chi. If building a new wall or fence, they can be dealt with by incorporating two pillars or gateposts to form an arrow which directs the sha chi back at the offending object. If keeping the existing fence, then we could plant two fairly substantial shrubs for the same effect.

EXTERNAL TO INTERNAL

Having taken account of the four animal directions in the surrounding environment, we can now begin to move inwards, taking a closer look at the internal boundaries of the plot area itself.

*Secure boundaries are important in Feng Shui. In a
large garden, a solid door in this wall, locked at night,
will increase the feeling of security.*

THE BOUNDARIES

TORTOISE

It is advisable to have a solid wall or substantial fence in this vulnerable position. Local authorities may have height restrictions on fences, so we can increase it by erecting trellis with climbing plants. Although prickly plants would seem to be useful in such a position, plants like pyracantha and holly tend to be slow-growing, and in this instance we need to create the barrier quickly. *Clematis montana* would be useful here, as would honeysuckle.

TIGER
— Back Garden —

Again, a fairly solid fence is required here, as there are communal gardens with open access to the street. Since we have identified this as an area with potential geopathic stress, dowsing will pinpoint places where some plants are unlikely to grow (*see Bibliography on page 125 for references on dowsing*). This fence is north-facing, and we should be aware of the limitations on plant choice. Branches of the elder trees which brush the fence and garage roof should be removed to avoid damage.

— Front Garden —

Symphoricarpus albus from next door has grown right up to the paving and overhangs the garage door. This can either be a battle or we can go with the flow. We can restrict the plant's relentless march by burying some up-ended paving slabs along the boundary. The foliage will still hang over, but away from the garage door. Underplanting with evergreen ground-cover plants will create a virtually maintenance-free

We need to investigate the four animals in the wider environment and within our own plot to ensure a harmonious space.

bed. The large sycamore tree by the driveway entrance is demolishing the fence and its roots are breaking up the paving. It will constantly seed itself and become a never-ending problem. It is also restricts the view of the road, which can be dangerous when driving out of the gate, thus it would be best to remove it.

DRAGON
— Back Garden —

This fence need not be as substantial as the others since it borders the neighbours' garden. We need to observe what is growing there and take it into account when designing. Overhanging trees will cause shade and will drip rainwater on to the plants beneath, which may protest. Rampant climbers will entangle themselves in shrubs and will need constant trimming, so we will need to bear access to the fence in mind. Plant roots coming through from next door may need containing.

— Front Garden —

The privet hedge will require trimming at least three times in the growing season, so it must be accessible. The existing narrow bed will not support many plants, since the privet will use all the soil moisture.

PHOENIX

There is tendency to plant tall shrubs in this position for privacy, but their size means they would use up most of the nutrients and moisture in the beds. Since the front garden slopes downwards, water will run away, so keep this in mind when designing beds.

HARMONIOUS SPACE

As we have seen, the plot is an irregular shape. We can use trellis, hedges, walls or shrubs in the garden to create regularity. The missing part of the house can be 'filled in', but in order not to obstruct the view from the window and to facilitate the maintenance of drains, we need to allow access. A pergola may be suitable here, or planting troughs, or we might place a pole or light in a position that will 'square off' the building.

CHI FLOW

The flow of chi will determine the shapes of the paths and beds. The most efficient way for the car to enter the property is straight into the garage, and so the driveway may be straight. If there is room, a turning point is useful and this can be built into the plan. The existing path to the front door creates sha chi since it points straight from the street. By altering the position of the front gate we can allow the path to meander to the door and deal with the tree and lamp-post opposite at the same time.

Since the front door is close to the fence, it feels restricted. We can alter this by creating a *Ming Tang* in front of the house (*see page* 53). This can be done by making an open space with paving, perhaps bordered by brick to distinguish it from the rest of the path. Pots on either side of the door will act as guardians and, if the plants in them are well maintained, will provide a healthy, welcoming entrance to the house. We have

already discussed the need to create space between the garage and the house, so we can devise a pleasant route between the two.

As the number of cars per household increases, more and more front gardens are being used as space for parking the cars. In some instances the cars even block access to the front door. If we do this, we not only restrict access to the house but also, symbolically, within our lives, since we have brought the outside world right inside our house. The car is the first thing we see, and smell, when we open the door and when we draw the curtains in the morning, and the last thing we see at night. Thus, if possible, we should attempt to create a *Ming Tang* outside the door at least, if not in front of the whole house, to enable us to relax.

While we are physically aware of the wind gusting round the side of a building and can see leaves spiralling around in corners, we may not be so aware of the psychological effect of less obvious energetic disturbances in the environment – the straight lines and points, creating the sha and cutting chi.

If we are aware of the local weather conditions and of the direction of the prevailing winds, then we can ensure that we have erected appropriate wind barriers. A hedge or permeable fence will slow the wind considerably for some distance beyond it, but will still allow the chi to flow through. Remember that the prevailing winds in the northern

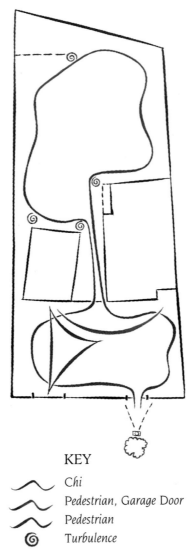

KEY

~ *Chi*
~ *Pedestrian, Garage Door*
~ *Pedestrian*
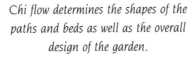 *Turbulence*

Chi flow determines the shapes of the paths and beds as well as the overall design of the garden.

hemisphere are north-easterly and south-westerly; in the southern hemisphere they are south-easterly and north-westerly. Large trees and buildings can alter the flow in places, and it is as well to be aware of this and also of the areas of shadow that they cast.

CLEARING THE SITE

This is decision time; the moment when we remove all the features that will stand in the way of us achieving the garden we really want. A garden is a controlled environment. If we had no control over our environment we would still be living in swamps and forests. If we can accept this fact and work with nature within our own space, then that is the best we can achieve. This will enable us to accept, in turn, that just because a tree is a tree it does not mean we have to keep it if it will create problems for us. We can always replace it with a more suitable one, but do check first to see if there are any Tree Protection Orders existing in your area.

An old tree will have built up a special relationship with its environment and be home to many creatures. We will have to be aware of this if we remove it, and attempt to recreate natural habitats for the displaced wildlife. Also, as the roots rot down, the surrounding land will sink and therefore need attention. Or, if we move the location of a pond, we will need first to have made adequate provisions for the frogs, toads, newts and other creatures that live there. They will not sit quietly, motionless, in the washing-up bowl while we dig the new hole!

How many of us struggle on with rockeries full of ground elder or couch grass, or the roots of a plant in the wrong place? If it causes us problems, then it should go – and we can always recreate it again, weed-free, or put it elsewhere. The plants which send suckers up everywhere should come out, or, if we really love them, may be replanted somewhere more suitable. The broken greenhouse we have been meaning to repair, which is casting shade on the vegetable garden; the unattractive

Trellis can act as a useful boundary or screen. Careful selection of plants is necessary, particularly on the border of a neighbour's garden. Open trellis filters the wind and slows it down, and can act as protection for plants.

pond in the wrong place; the paving which had been laid wrongly at the side of the house and which irritates us each time we go out of the kitchen door; the broken paving and steps in the back garden and the crazy paving in the front; the lumpy lawn which is bare and never grows, or the lawn which grows too fast in places that the mower will not touch; and the thousand-and-one other features we would not choose to live with, if only … We can do something now and take charge of our lives to create the harmonious space which will nourish us.

GARDEN FEATURES

UTILITIES AND STORAGE

Using permaculture methods will ensure that the most-used features are placed near the house. We will need a space for dustbins and storage space for tools. Sowing and potting areas should be close to the main growing area and a water supply. The space between the house and the garage accommodates all these features as well as water-butts which catch rainwater from the garage, shed and potting-bench roofs. Fresh water for seedlings and pots can be provided from an outside tap.

A greenhouse and cold frames are essential parts of a kitchen garden and should be close to a water supply. Lean-to greenhouses and frames take up less space and are located here along the back wall of the garage (*see right*).

KITCHEN AND HERB GARDENS

We often find the kitchen or herb garden tucked away out of sight and consequently forgotten for a large part of the year. Ideally it should be situated near the kitchen door, and accessible without walking on the soil. The Feng Shui kitchen garden will be as beautiful as the rest of the garden, so it will not need hiding away. Kitchen gardens are best orientated on a north–south axis so they can benefit from the sun throughout the day. Extra water-butts can catch the rain from the roof of the house and make it available to the kitchen garden via a leaky-pipe system.

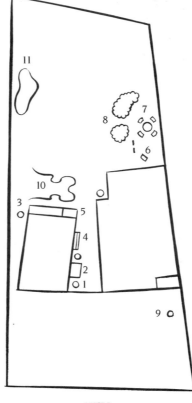

KEY

1 Dustbin • 2 Shed • 3 Water-butts
4 Potting bench • 5 Greenhouse/cold frame • 6 Seating area • 7 Social seating area • 8 Shrubs to screen seating area
9 Water feature/small fountain
10 Kitchen-garden keyhole beds for easy access • 11 Pond

Being aware of the chi flow helps us design the features in the garden and place them harmoniously.

SEATING

We have already identified the area of geopathic stress, and it is advisable not to place seating here. Our tranquil space will be screened from the windows in the apartment block opposite using plant-covered trellis. A social seating area where we may eat in the summer should ideally be near to the kitchen. In this garden the drains are close by, so a better place is at the back of the house. Since food will have to be carried through the house or the garden, routes should be clear. We can screen this area, too, and create a dining room within the garden.

WATER

Water can fulfil several functions in the garden. A pond can attract wildlife – dragonflies and frogs, which clear up the insect pests, and birds and small animals, which come to the pond to drink. The sound of running water can be soothing and it can energize an enclosed space, or we can use it transcendentally to attract good fortune. The wildlife pond should create as natural an environment as possible for the creatures we wish to visit it, and should not be too accessible to their predators. The ideal pond shape will have as much surface area as possible since, as we have seen, chi accumulates where two landforms meet. To attract our 'helpful friends' we need to provide them with as many habitats as we can. Remember that square shapes should be avoided because of the points

ABOVE. *Ponds attract wildlife, which needs plant cover for shelter. In this pond, the rocks are too steep to allow frogs and toads to use the pond freely.*

RIGHT. *The sound of running water can be soothing, but are we really comfortable near a creature which constantly spouts water from its mouth – surely an act that is far from natural?*

and straight lines. Circles, on the other hand, have the least circumference of all the shapes, and so a meandering shape is best.

A small water feature in or near our quiet garden will sooth us as we unwind, and, since it is close to the house, access to electricity for the pump will not be a problem. As we saw on pages 56–7, the east is an auspicious position for water until the year 2003. To improve our fortunes, therefore, a well-maintained water feature in the front garden, which faces east in our example, would be a good idea.

SHAPES AND MATERIALS

Having made the boundaries secure, taken steps to protect against creeping roots from outside, removed some features and selected suitable sites for others, we are now ready to create the beds and paths. The chi flow will virtually have decided this for us, but it remains for us to decide on the exact shapes and materials we wish to use.

THE BORDERS

Since the front garden slopes slightly, we need to ensure that water and soil do not run away by building low retaining walls or using edging materials. The door area is restricted, and taking the path close to the fence would compound this problem as well as leave a narrow bed by the privet hedge. It is preferable to swing the path the other way, which will help to draw the entrance more into the centre, leaving a wider border by the fence. In a suburban area, the fence between the front of the house and the garage is vulnerable, and it would add to security if a prickly plant were planted here. Pyracantha grows reasonably fast, but not so fast as to restrict the gate. Holly is slower-growing, but in time would deter any opportunist. Prickly plants are a nuisance if we allow them to be, but they also have their uses.

THE ENTRANCE

Because of the restriction it is important to create as wide an entrance as possible. We can give the front door its own *Ming Tang* by using materials here which make it stand out from the rest of the paving

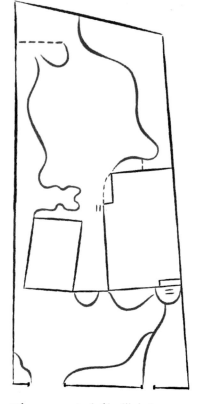

The movement of chi will design our paths and borders for us, as we have seen. We should make sure that the materials we use blend in with the house and the local environment.

– for example, a semicircular brick area edged with an up-ended brick or one of a different colour, or a gravel area edged with brick. The bed in front of the house can follow the contours of the chi flow.

MATERIALS

The materials we choose should be durable and low-maintenance, and fit not only into the colour scheme and five-element cycle of our own environment, but also complement the wider environment in general. It is one thing to be individual but quite another to be at odds with the environment, and we can express our individuality by creating a wonderful garden.

We can choose from paving slabs, brick and a host of other materials for the drive. Gravel is another option, although not practical where the ground slopes. Where it is useful is at the side of the house, which, as already suggested, might be vulnerable. We might also choose to use gravel instead of grass, or we could choose to cut down on the mowing by creating a wildflower lawn (*see right*). Alternatives are camomile or even paving – but, in a garden growing vegetables, grass clippings are a useful addition to the compost heap since they enable it to heat up quickly, which increases the chance of any weed seeds in it being destroyed. Also, we need not use up precious water resources maintaining the lawn: clever utilization of bath water (though not the perfumed variety!) and leaky pipes buried beneath the lawn will save both water and labour.

THE COMPOST HEAP

An afterthought? Not at all. Compost heaps are the most important feature in the garden for the organic grower. They are usually where we would expect them to be, tucked out of sight, but in this garden this is actually the prime position (*see garden plan on pages 88–9*). If we superimpose the template of the Bagua over the plot, we will see that the wealth area is extended, and the compost bins are situated in this area. The nutrients which plants and vegetables remove from the soil can be recycled back into it: uncooked vegetative waste, hair, brown paper and cardboard – even old woollen socks – can be returned to the soil to enrich it. Within these bins is the substance which will make our gardens productive, our plants healthy and our crops health-giving, and which will ultimately create an environment in which we can be truly happy.

LEFT. *This garden incorporates gravel and camomile areas, both of which may be used as low-maintenance substitutes for grass.*

BELOW. *Lawns can be time-consuming if we let them be. This lawn is allowed to run free in places, and thus blends harmoniously with the border.*

Design

*Now that we have removed all the unwanted features
and taken note of those which will affect us in the
wider environment, we can begin to design our garden.*

We have seen that change is both desirable and inevitable, so we should not be concerned at making changes as we proceed, although if we have designed with the flow of the garden and the activities which are to be carried out in it, these changes will be minimal.

If we follow permaculture rules, everything will have more than one function. There will still be room for the merely gorgeous – the pot we adore or the garishly painted table. These things will make the garden special for us. Features we have compromised on because they were in a sale or on special offer, or a present we hate but feel obliged to use, we will not grow to love but rather will always resent. It is best to let them go and choose things to make our garden a special place.

Redesigning the Garden According to Feng Shui Principles

•1 The brick pillars add stability to this low wall and act as guardians.

•2 The tree on the other side of the road is still overpowering; a Fire-shaped obelisk positioned here will give the illusion of reducing its size and will symbolically 'burn' the wood.

•3 A small water feature here will add the 'lucky' water aspect to the garden, beneficial until the year 2023.

•4 The house faces east which is the Wood element. A Wood feature, perhaps some wooden planters on either side of the entrance, will highlight the element.

•5 We need access to this wide bed, and a small open area will enable us to reach all parts of it.

•6 This Ming Tang welcomes residents and visitors.

•7 A light here 'raises up' the slope.

•8 These water-butts will help us to conserve water.

•9 A gravel path from the back gate encircling the garage will deter intruders, as will a prickly hedge.

•10 The dustbins are positioned near the gate for convenience.

•11 A large lidded bucket will store household vegetable waste, to be taken to the compost heaps later.

•12 Vegetables are planted north–south to receive maximum light. Keyhole shapes allow for ease of access.

•13 A slow-growing conifer offers privacy from the windows in the apartment block.

•14 The pergola fills in the missing space and allows a short cut to the garden table.

•15 Shrubs offer privacy for the patio.

•16 A private place for quiet relaxation at the end of a long day. A small water feature will soothe.

•17 The utility areas are tucked away but also easily accessible.

•18 The pond – now a more natural shape – is situated in between the vegetable garden and the compost heap, where some of our 'helpful people' reside.

•19 The trellis has an arbour built in. Not a comfortable area in which to sit, with the compost heaps behind, but a large urn can be striking here and can symbolize waiting for the 'wealth' to pour in.

•20 The roots of this tree are to be encouraged. Elder roots growing through compost speed up the decaying process and provide a wonderful crumbly mixture. Now the large tree has gone, the elder will grow and act as a wind filter on the corner of the apartment block.

•21 Climbers on the trellis will deter intruders.

•22 A tall plant in a tub on this corner will shield the kitchen from a 'poison arrow' and cut down wind turbulence.

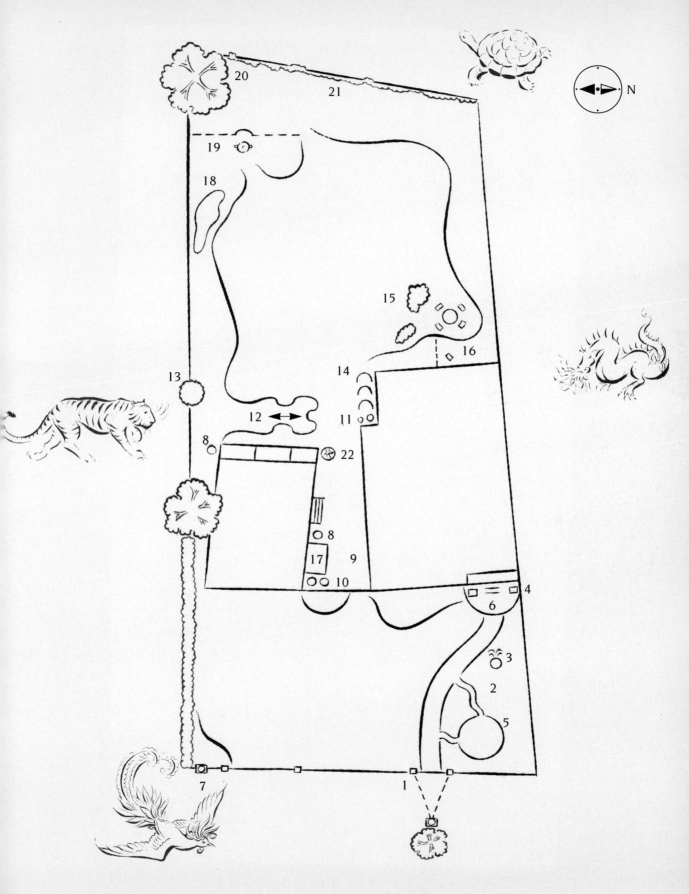

The Bagua as a Design Tool

The Bagua enables us to reflect in our homes and gardens
what we want from our lives. By working with the energies
it identifies how we can create the lives we desire.

We have seen that the Bagua is a template, recently introduced to represent the Later Heaven sequence, and designed to enable us to encourage chi to flow freely through our homes. When we superimpose the Bagua on to any area, we are representing the journey of life. To encourage a smooth flow of chi is to create a smooth path through life. To be aware of our position in the swirling forces of the universe and harmonize those forces around us brings health, wealth and happiness.

POSITIONING THE BAGUA

First position the Bagua over the whole plot, so that we enter through any one of the three 'Gates of Chi' – that is, through the Knowledge, Career or Helpful People areas, or those marked 8, 1 and 6 on the Bagua. The Bagua should be positioned so that these areas are placed at the entrance to a house or area of the garden. If your main entrance is on the side of the plot, then the Bagua is turned round so that the Gate of Chi sits in one of these three areas. The Bagua can then be superimposed over the plot, the house, or over each area in the garden, being positioned over each section at the point of entry, as shown in the diagram to the right.

A small extension, as shown in Diagram 1 (*right*), is seen as a projection of that area and may increase the energy there. If there is a large area missing, as in Diagram 2 (*right*), then a sector of the Bagua is missing and we will need to take steps to remedy the situation by applying an appropriate enhancement as shown on the following pages. The ideal plot is one in which each sector of the Bagua is complete. In the example shown in Diagram 2, for instance, we should aim to create the illusion that the missing area exists by using a mirror or *trompe l'oeil*.

Regard the Bagua as flexible. It will sit on your plot whether it is long and thin, or very wide. We can create regular shapes within irregular plots using plants, hedges or trellis. Using the Bagua colours, which are based on the five elements, or the elemental shapes, we can build up beneficial vibrations in each sector which combine to form a harmonious whole.

On the five-element table of correspondences (*see page* 25) we saw that each section of the Bagua is related to an element and to a part of the body. With some knowledge of herbal medicine it is therefore possible to plant herbs in a beneficial spot.

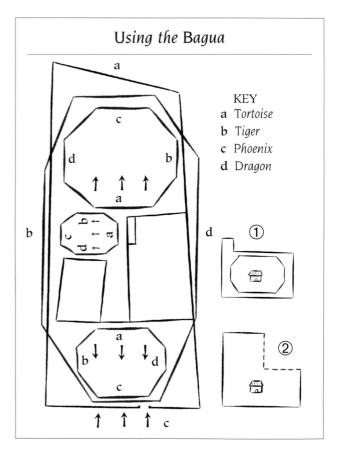

Using the Bagua

KEY
a Tortoise
b Tiger
c Phoenix
d Dragon

BAGUA: THE JOURNEY

The categories allocated to each section of the Bagua can help us to investigate the vibrational energies that are present there. Pages 94–5 indicate the Feng Shui enhancements (such as light, colour and movement) which can be used to increase or improve the energies in a given sector. Chi always moves in a particular sequence through an environment, beginning with the Career, or Journey, sector.

CAREER OR JOURNEY

Career can literally mean our job prospects, but it can also mean the passage of life, with the infinite possibilities it offers. There are often obstacles in our way – either of our own making, or ones that we perceive others have placed there for us. In this area, we need a clear passage in order to open up the endless opportunities ahead. Overhanging branches and prickles which snare our clothes have no place here. Squeaking hinges on a gate will irritate us as we enter and remind us of jobs not yet done. Overgrown flowerbeds or cars parked outside the front door present us with obstacles each time we enter our private space.

A splash of colour, long-lived plants, a meandering pathway and the prospect of something beyond …
The journey begins.

If we create an unrestricted entrance, psychologically we have created the possibility to move on in life. The colour associated with this area is black or dark blue and the element is Water.

RELATIONSHIPS

The Relationships area can encompass partnerships, but also friendships and relationships with colleagues. Not the area for single items, we should aim for groups of plants or, if partnerships are a priority, pairs of shrubs or pots, or perhaps a statue of two figures. Pink is often associated with this area, although yellow would also be suitable since the element is Earth.

ELDERS OR FAMILY

This represents our ancestors, those we admire and also ancient wisdom. It is the place for an elderly relative's cottage in a large plot, and an ideal spot for the greenhouse or nursery bed, where seedlings are sown in the time-honoured method with regard to the moon. A garden table here, where the family come together to eat, is another option. The colour associated with this area is green and the element is Wood.

AREA, COLOUR AND ELEMENT

Career or Journey

One of the Gates of Chi, this represents life's journey. In the Water element, the colours are black and dark blue.

Relationships

This is in the Earth element. Sometimes the Bagua is regarded as a colour wheel, and then pink is used in this area.

Elders or Family

This is in the Wood element and is represented by the colour green.

WEALTH

Wealth usually denotes finance, but if health is poor, money becomes meaningless. In the garden, the wealth area is ideal for compost heaps, rich in the substance which sustains the soil and, consequently, us. An empty urn in this area invites our desires to pour in, provided our intentions are honourable. Greed will rebound on us, since when yang reaches its ultimate position it changes to its opposite. The colour associated with this area is blue (sometimes purple) and the element is Wood.

TAI CHI

The Tai Chi area is the 'Great Void'. It is a space which allows the chi to return and be replenished, and then move on. It represents an opening for infinite possibilities, and thus the area should be kept clear. If we allow a central space in our garden, we allow the free flow of energy and are not channelling it away too quickly. The element associated with this area is Earth, and the Earth colours are yellow or gold, orange and brown.

HELPFUL PEOPLE

Birds are 'helpful people', since they keep down garden pests. Shrubs or bird boxes for nesting would be suitable here. A sculpture or object pertaining to a focus in our lives would be appropriate. A statue of a Buddha for Buddhists, a Gaia figure for ecologists or representations of deities all have a place here. The colours associated with this area are white and silver, and the element is Metal.

ABOVE. *The earth goddess goes well in the Helpful People area.*

FAR LEFT. *An empty urn enables the universe to fill it with what we desire .*

LEFT. *With no Tai Chi area, chi is endlessly funnelled on a long, uphill path.*

AREA, COLOUR AND ELEMENT

Wealth	Tai Chi	Helpful People
We encourage life's riches to pour in here. The element is Wood and the colours blue or purple.	Plants will be healthier where we leave space for the air to circulate. This is the Earth element, and the colours yellow and gold.	One of the Gates of Chi, this is the Metal element and the colours are white and silver.

CREATIVE OR OFFSPRING

This can represent children, special projects or things we have made. A children's play area with a metal climbing frame would be suitable, as would a special plant collection, a workshop, home-made pots or a set of garden sculptures. The element for this area is Metal, and the colours white or silver.

KNOWLEDGE

Knowledge may be that which we already possess, or that which we are seeking. Seedlings, vegetables and flowers may be cultivated here. This area would also be suitable for a meditation garden, a place where we can relax. The colour blue is often associated with this area, although yellow would also be appropriate since its element is Earth.

We all need space to unwind, to think, to read or simply to be still. If every one of us had a space like this, the world would be a much calmer place.

FAME

Fame signifies our accomplishments. It does not mean that we have achieved notoriety, but if we have become a famous sculptor then this is the place for our finest work. We will have achieved something along the way and gained insight. A Moon Gate here will allow us to glimpse the possibilities to come in the next stage. The colour associated with this area is red and its element is Fire.

CREATE A SPECIAL PLACE

The diagram shows how chi moves through an environment. We can make our garden special by making the journey, either by walking it through or standing at the front gate and visualizing it. As we follow the route we should, if the garden is designed well, move freely. In each sector we can think of its meaning – about our friends and family, our projects and our aspirations and the things we have yet to learn. Back at the beginning, we will hopefully be wiser and ready for the next stage. This is known as 'Walking the Nine Palaces'.

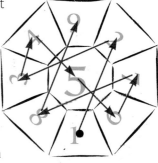

Having created this special place, we may want to protect it. A transcendental protection ritual involves moving to each corner of your plot and imagining a protective shield of white light encircling the garden to guard it against negative forces from the outside world.

AREA, COLOUR AND ELEMENT

Creative or Offspring	*Knowledge*	*Fame*
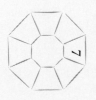 Our children or projects are represented here. It is the Metal element, and the colours are white and silver.	 This is a Gate of Chi, representing what we know or seek. The Earth element in this area is associated with the colour blue.	The fulfilment of our aims and goals, this is the Fire element and the colour is red.

THE EIGHT ENHANCEMENTS

The enhancements are instruments which we can use to connect ourselves to the energy of a particular space. They work transcendentally, and by focusing on a particular area of our life as symbolized by the Bagua we can hope to activate the energy there and bring about change.

• *Light* • We can use actual lights to illuminate an area, or we can use reflection or borrowed light (from the view) instead. A lamp or garden torch placed in the Career area may help us at an interview. If a space is 'missing' from the garden, then a strategically placed mirror reflecting a meandering path will imply that the space is there. A 'borrowed view' through a Moon Gate in a hedge will energize a dark corner.

• *Sound* • Nature's own sounds are best in the garden. If we provide a protective environment for songbirds, the air will be filled with song; if crows or magpies prey on them, the sounds will be very different. To activate a space we can plant bamboo, which rustles gently in the breeze. The sound of trickling water can enhance an area.

LEFT. *Bamboo is as much at home in Western as in Eastern gardens. The gentle swishing noise it makes in the wind, or as we brush past, can be energizing.*

ABOVE. *The sozu when full of water tips with a clonking noise. Invented by a Zen priest in order to hear the silence more clearly, it was carefully crafted to 'clonk' every twenty minutes. Modern versions are more regular, and can be irritating.*

• **Colour** • If we want to focus on a particular area, a simple method is by placing something relating to the colour of the sector of the Bagua in the required spot to enhance it (*see below right*).

• **Life** • In a house, this usually means a fish tank. There should be life already in the garden if we have designed it well. A bird box would help to enhance the Helpful People area.

• **Movement** • Water is a useful tool for this. The size of the water feature should be In proportion to its situation; bigger does not always mean better. Weather-vanes are another way to introduce movement. Swaying plants can also move energy on.

• **Mechanical Devices** • An extension of movement, these could include ornaments which move in the wind and water pumps. In positioning them we should not interfere with the natural processes.

• **Stillness** • Rocks and statues come into this category and will make more of an impact if they have relevance for us. A large limestone rock will be a powerful enhancement for a Zen priest, but others may prefer a statue or sculpture.

• **Straight Lines** • Although straight lines usually suggest sha chi in Feng Shui, they can sometimes be used to move energy on. In the Barbican in London, coloured lines on the walkways direct pedestrians through the maze of buildings to the theatre, the local school and other places. In the garden we can use a stretch of straight path or a wooden handrail to move the energy on quickly through an area.

BELOW. *Water will energize any space. A gentle bubbling noise lifts our spirits and refreshes us, whereas rushing water exhausts us.*

BELOW. *A splash of colour can draw our attention and stand out vividly against a natural background.*

Paths and Entrances

*First impressions are important, both for
ourselves and for our visitors. Well-maintained
paths and entrances can welcome us home,
while messy ones can dull our spirits.*

PATHS

Straight paths hurry us through the garden. Meandering paths, on the other hand, slow us down and allow us to take in our surroundings. They also facilitate the smooth flow of chi. If a path is too narrow, the plants will brush against our ankles. If plants near the path are too high, they will overwhelm us; if they are too wide and sprawling, we will constantly need to trim them back from the path; and if they smell unpleasant, then they will deter us from walking there.

Paths need to go to somewhere. If a path does not lead to a gate, for instance, a circular route is preferable to a dead end. The materials used for the path should be firm. Paving slabs and gravel are reliable, but cobblestones and worn bricks are unstable. Grass will get muddy and need constant attention. A lawnmower can move freely if the path is slightly lower than the grass, saving us endless time trimming the edges. Another factor to bear in mind is that a path gently sloping away from the house will allow rainwater to run away.

ABOVE. *This bark path meanders gently
through the garden and offers a glimpse
of the space beyond.*

LEFT. *Two clipped mounds guard the house
opposite, while the gateposts deflect the
sha chi from the tree. The path meanders
gently to the front door. A broad-leaved
plant by the gate would improve the
yin–yang balance and prevent ankles
being tickled on the way through.*

ENTRANCES

The entrance is the first thing we see when we arrive home, and also the first glimpse our visitors have from which to gain an impression. A well-maintained, attractive entrance is welcoming, whereas a dark, gloomy or messy entrance affects our moods and our energy. Some Chinese buildings have guardians at the entrance – often dragons or other symbolic animals. Larger houses elsewhere may have a pair of lions gracing the entrance. However humble our home, we too can have guardians. A pair of stone pots will serve this purpose well. The entrance should not be restricted, and plant tendrils hanging down from porches can be disconcerting, particularly at night. Also, prickly plants are not a good idea, since they snag our clothes and do not create a friendly welcome.

Many large houses have multiple occupancy. Unlike apartment blocks, which have maintenance

The lines and colours are all Earth here, with two Metal-shaped plants acting as guardians. Small Fire-shaped obelisks or trees would enliven the chi of this otherwise charming entrance.

contracts for tidying up the grounds, in converted houses often no one is directly responsible for the upkeep of the garden. Consequently, such gardens can become overgrown and shabby. A positive gesture to clear the garden will probably be met, in turn, with positive gestures from the other tenants. Complaints, on the other hand, will merely engender negative feedback. Even if you are the only volunteer, you will feel better about your home. A common sight in such houses is a row of rubbish bins in the front garden. If there is nowhere else to put them, they should be screened and kept tidy. Piles of free newspapers and circulars may also clutter up the entrance; individual mailboxes in the entrance hall can alleviate this problem.

Buildings and Structures

*Buildings and structures should be in proportion
to the size of the garden and be easily accessible.
They should be well maintained, and fit into
the space harmoniously.*

If we employ permaculture techniques in the garden, then any building or structure should be useful and fulfil a number of functions. For example, a shed will not only store tools, but also enable us to collect rainwater. We might be able to attach a nesting box to it, and it will provide support for climbing plants or protection for delicate ones. If the garden shed is at the end of the garden this creates a psychological barrier to walking to it to collect the lawnmower or tools. If it is close to the house, however, it means that we may constantly think of jobs that we could do in a spare moment. Greenhouses and cold frames need to be located close to a water supply in order to be utilized properly.

Pergolas can provide support, not only for flowering climbers but also for food plants like runner beans. They can provide welcome shade over terraces and are almost essential in hot climates. Small arbours can shelter us from the wind and provide a cocoon-like haven where we can escape to unwind.

EFFECTS ON THE ENVIRONMENT

When we erect a building or a structure, it is good practice to think of the effect it will have on the existing environment. Will it create shade where there was none before, and what effect will that have on the plants in the area? Is it likely that a fox might dig underneath it? Would this matter, or would it upset the balance of the ecosystem – and if so, should we plan ahead to prevent it by sinking a barrier below the ground? As we build, it is useful to check if any points or corners are likely to send 'poison arrows' towards the house or the seating areas in the garden.

We also need to bear in mind that the colour and shape of a structure can affect the balance of the elements, so we may need to take steps to regain that balance. However, since the Feng Shui garden is, after all, a tranquil and harmonious place, we do not need to think in practical terms all the time. We can express ourselves freely in the garden. A beautiful building, a grotto, a mosaic wall, a painted pot, an interesting rock or an artefact from a favourite place or treasured time can create a place which is very special for us. Another way to personalize our space outside as well as inside the house is by using coloured wood stains.

ABOVE. *This greenhouse fits perfectly into this small courtyard garden, although the cat stalking the birds on the roof is an unnecessary feature.*

RIGHT. *This wisteria-covered pergola will provide protection from the hot sun as well as offering a wonderful scented retreat in the corner of the garden.*

Seats and Statues

Where we place ourselves in the garden and the images with which we surround ourselves can subconsciously have a profound effect on our feeling of well-being.

SEATS

Whether we are sunbathing, reading or simply watching the children play, we need to feel as comfortable and at ease in the garden as we do inside the house. It is advisable to position seats so that we can sit on them without feeling vulnerable; a path behind us can make us feel as if someone is creeping up on us. If there is a fence behind the seat, whether we are cat lovers or not, the scrabbling and sudden appearance of our neighbour's intrepid mouser perched precariously on the fence above our head is not conducive to a feeling of tranquillity!

The armchair shape of the Tortoise, Dragon and Tiger is in evidence here. The watering can would be best moved elsewhere, or it will be a constant reminder of a job that needs doing.

Seats can be positioned using the classic Form School Dragon, Tiger and Tortoise – or armchair – formation. The fourth, or Phoenix, position in front of the seat should have an open aspect. This provides the occupant with a secure, comfortable feeling as well as a pleasant view. Seats with high backs and arms have a built-in Tortoise, Dragon and Tiger. Overhanging plants with loose tendrils or the downward-pointing branches of a tree can be a nuisance and can also startle us, particularly at dusk. Spiked plants pointing at us can cause sha chi, and prickles that catch clothing and scratch us can make us feel both uncomfortable and irritable.

Being aware of the shapes and colours which surround the seat will enable us to ensure that the five elements are in harmony. Fire-shaped obelisks or conifers, or red and orange planting around the patio dining table would not make for harmonious conversation with dinner guests on a summer's evening, and may even lead to arguments. On the other hand, green leafy planting in swirly Water-shaped beds, with the gentle ripple of water over pebbles, would not be right in an area where we are supervising children on climbing frames or keeping an eye on toddlers playing near the fish pond, since we may drift off into quiet meditation instead of remaining alert.

STATUES

The images with which we surround ourselves in our homes and gardens can affect us subconsciously and are more often than not an indication of our mood or state of mind. The more we become aware of the patterns we establish for ourselves, the better equipped we will be to bring about positive changes to the areas of our lives we are not happy with. If we sit in the garden surrounded by beautiful images, then we will feel at peace and in a happy frame of mind. A fierce image, on the other hand, will disconcert or even scare us. Human shapes in statues are difficult if they are isolated in the middle of an open space: to look out of a window at night and see a human form can be frightening. Statues of famous people who have achieved great things in life can also be difficult in a garden. To sit close to them will remind us of all the things we have not done.

RIGHT. *Imagine trying to relax in the garden alongside this statue. It might act as a deterrent to the neighbour's cat, or even act as a scarecrow, but it will not allow us to relax and feel at ease. Nor, indeed, will the fiery planting.*

BELOW. *In these gloriously tranquil, relaxing surroundings there is nothing to suggest that life is anything but wonderful.*

Window Boxes

*In an apartment, a window box may be our only
planting space. We can use it to lift the chi or to
focus on a particular area of our life. We can also
grow herbs for culinary or health purposes.*

If you live in an apartment there may not be any access to a garden, so you will need to make use of the growing space that a window box provides. Depending on your focus, you can use the planting to lift your spirits or to calm you down, to improve your health or to concentrate your thoughts on a certain aspect of your life. Use slow-growing perennial plants where possible, since they consume less time and energy than annuals and will last for several seasons. It can be useful to leave the plants in their pots and stand them in the window box. This will allow for plants which have died or outgrown their space to be replaced easily.

THE FIVE ELEMENTS

Consider the five-element cycles (*see page* 24) when choosing plants, and take the colour of the walls, sills and any other paintwork into consideration. Elemental shapes should also be taken into account (the shape of the planting shown here is Earth, for instance), not forgetting any shapes which are part of the design of the building and window-sill edging.

PLANTING FOR MOOD AND EMOTIONS

The colours we wear and surround ourselves with have a profound effect on our chi. The vibrational energy of colour affects us visually, subconsciously and through our emotions. If we are happy and healthy then there is much to be said for planting our window boxes with the plants and colours we like. Herbs, as well as being pleasant to look at, smell wonderful and taste delicious. Basil, chives, chervil, dill, lemon balm, mint, oregano, sage and tarragon all grow well in pots. Consult the companion-planting table (*see pages* 118–123) to see if any do not grow well with each other.

PLANTING FOR FOCUS AND HEALTH
~ The Bagua ~

It is possible to use window boxes to focus on areas of the Bagua. Place the Bagua over the window box so that the Gates of Chi are the nearest sectors to you as you look out from the window (*see also page* 90). Use plants which correspond to the colour of the area you wish to focus on.

~ The Five Elements ~

The window box is simply a mini-garden, and we can use the five elements in the same way as we can in a much larger environment (*see page* 24–31).

ABOVE. *A useful mix of perennial evergreen and annual plants. Wood (plants) and Earth (trough, pattern on blinds, shape of planting) are represented. A small Fire-shaped tree in the centre would make all the difference.*

RIGHT. *This planting would act as a focus in the wealth area. It would, however, add too much Fire energy outside the kitchen and be too enlivening for a bedroom window – some Metal (white) and Wood (green foliage) would tone it down.*

Roof Gardens, Balconies, Terraces

*The same Feng Shui rules apply whether we have
a large estate or a small roof garden or terrace.
We have to be mindful of the needs of the plants
we choose, but we use the same principles to
create a peaceful haven for ourselves.*

The first consideration when designing a roof garden or a balcony is safety. We have to be aware of what we are placing above our neighbours' heads; a large number of balconies jut out from buildings with no visible means of support, so we have to consider carefully the weight of the materials and objects we use. If the balcony is strong enough, large terracotta pots or stones in the front corners symbolically 'ground' it. Roof gardens are already grounded, but need very supportive barriers. Flooring is important, particularly since the plants will require a lot of watering due to the effects of the sun and drying winds, and it should be well maintained and feel stable. The next factor is direction. A south- or west-facing balcony or roof garden with sea views has a very different feel to a balcony at the back of an apartment block which looks out on to a rock face or a roof garden amid skyscrapers.

PLANTS

Remember that heavy pruning is not advised in Feng Shui. Recommended plants are those which last more than one season and those which are slow-growing. The plants we choose should reflect the particular location, and the colours we use should follow the sequence of the five elements (*see pages* 24–31). Many balconies and roof gardens are Earth-shaped; a balance of elements can give even a modest space a lift. It is possible to grow vegetables, and fast-growing salad crops are particularly recommended. Herbs will fare well, too, since many of them do not require much watering. To minimize the watering, drought-resistant plants are preferable to those which are continually thirsty.

WIND

Wind can be a problem high up, and many plants are unable to cope with strong winds without adequate protection. Trellis, bamboo screens and wind-resistant plants can act as buffers. There is a danger that chi can become trapped if a space is enclosed on three sides, or can disperse too quickly if the sides are open. Careful planting can ensure that chi meanders gently. Be mindful of sharp edges from neighbouring buildings in an urban environment, and plant to hide them.

WATER

Sun-baked balconies or roof gardens and those exposed to drying winds may benefit from the installation of a small water feature to enliven the atmosphere and create a pleasant sound. A shallow dish with moist pebbles is another possibility.

A balcony or roof garden is not a natural environment, since plants do not naturally grow in containers up in the air, so we have to accept total responsibility for their well-being. The networks usually present in an ecosystem are absent, so an imbalance often occurs. Make every attempt, therefore, to buy healthy plants, and check for unwanted wildlife before incorporating them into your planting. Watering can also present problems. If a tap is available, a leaking-hose system can take the hard work out of watering and also safeguard downstairs neighbours from an unwanted evening shower. Pigeons can be a real problem on city balconies and roof gardens; shiny and moving objects can discourage them. If netting becomes essential, try to incorporate it into the design to prevent a feeling of being caged in.

TERRACES

Terraces are particularly popular in hot climates and are often covered by an awning or canopy where welcome shade is needed. In colder climates, terraces are usually left open to capture every possible moment of sunshine. They can be designed according to the Form School principles. Where there is a terrace, there is often a view, and we can cut down on work if we 'borrow' the view and keep container planting to a minimum. Again, as with roof gardens, careful choice of drought-resistant plants is advisable. Terraces are often home to a wide variety of activities; they can act as peaceful havens where we can sit and relax, as play areas for children, or perhaps as places for entertaining guests. Be mindful of the five-element cycles when designing the terrace, particularly when siting a barbecue.

ABOVE. *This balcony is surrounded by trees and could so easily be dark and lifeless. The use of lively features – the bird and the reflective ball – introduces some colour and elemental shapes. Low-maintenance plants and comfortable seating help to create a restful and intimate feel.*

RIGHT. *An alternative view of the city that never sleeps! The canopy of Central Park becomes part of this balcony garden and acts as its Ming Tang. It is hard to imagine that such an oasis exists in one of the most energetic cities in the world.*

Choosing Plants

*If we aim to know our plants and their needs and
to choose plants indigenous to the area, then we
will create a balanced and harmonious garden.*

Plants in the Feng Shui garden are chosen for longevity. The pine is always sited as a prime example, but few of us have a garden big enough to house such a large tree. Ideally, before we plant we should find out about the habits and potential size of the plants and trees we grow. What is a little tree now, because we clip it every week, may grow into a nuisance for our successors, who are unaware of its potential.

PLACEMENT

It is difficult to keep track of all the new varieties of plants available, but if we aim to create our garden with plants which are indigenous – not only to the country in which we live, but to the specific area of the country – then we are helping the plants to feel comfortable in their surroundings. To endeavour to grow a plant from a different climate causes stress both for the plant and for ourselves as we try to keep it alive. Knowledge of the preferred soil type of each plant, and of the particular environment in which it grows naturally, will help us to create the best conditions for it. Plants show signs of stress in

In this garden there is a balance of yin and yang and the five elements. Plants have been selected for longevity and all blend together harmoniously.

the wrong environment, just as we do, only they need our help to change location. The aim of Feng Shui is to maintain harmony in the wider environment, although individuality is always to be admired. A cactus garden in London is out of place, for example, as is a cottage garden in Kuala Lumpur.

In the natural world, plants rarely stand in splendid isolation but seed themselves in drifts. A single specimen tree can, however, seem timeless, and is regarded in a similar way to the large limestone rocks which stand in the great Chinese gardens. Colour in nature is subtle – and so too in the Feng Shui garden. A single bloom can be far more beautiful than a large expanse of gaudy hybrids. Even the giant cactus *Carnegiea gigantea* can be a thing of beauty, all twelve metres (forty feet) of it, in the right place, and the magnificent gunnera, which makes such a statement in damp environments, would look out of place in an average urban household garden.

PLANTS AND NEIGHBOURS

We have already addressed the dilemma of having something from which we want to shield ourselves quickly, and

LEFT. *This clematis will need constant attention to keep it in check. Once the flowers are over, the new growth will straggle everywhere, and in winter the dormant growth will not be attractive in this front garden.*

choosing a plant which will do the job admirably in the short term but prove to be a problem later on. A common instance where we are tempted to plant fast-growing plants is to shield ourselves form being overlooked. This is a problem particularly in urban areas, but to resist the temptation to plant *Clematis montana* or *Polygonum baldschuanicum*, the 'mile-a-minute' vine, is to remain on friendly terms with the neighbours and allow us some free time. To plant **x** *Cupressocyparis leylandii* in an urban space is a form of vandalism, and this thoughtless act will almost certainly lead to disputes with neighbours. Yet it is everywhere, affecting drains and taking moisture from neighbouring plants and lawns in its relentless march to the sky.

The importance of the seasons is, as we have seen, vital in Feng Shui. There is a right place and a right time for everything. A period of growth, bloom, seed and rest. Rest is not death and decay, but rather nurturing and gathering. Many seeds we buy from nurseries have to be placed in the refrigerator before planting to coax them into life. It is all part of the cycle. Pity, then, the supermarket bean, which spends its nights in a continent where it would not normally grow, under arc lights to bring it to our tables in double-quick time in the wrong season. Where is its life force and what life force does it pass on to us?

If we are mindful of the seasons and cycles, provide good neighbours and good nourishment for our plants and maintain balance and harmony among the five elements, and if we remember the maxim, 'the right place at the right time', we will not stray from the Way.

∽ CHOOSING PLANTS BY ELEMENT ∽

The following table offers suggestions of a variety of plants which are suitable for introducing a particular element into the garden. There are, of course, several factors which need to be considered — location, soil type, and the plant's habits, in particular, and these are indicated here. You need to be mindful, also, of a number of other aspects, such as whether a plant will fit into an existing plant scheme, whether it will have any affect on the overall yin–yang balance, whether it is sun-loving or prefers shade, the direction of the prevailing wind, if it needs staking, and other such considerations.

As you become familiar with using the elements, you will be able to sense what is missing and what is too abundant, and will intuitively choose plants to redress the balance. If you make mistakes, these can easily be rectified. Regard the plants below as examples and choose ones that you like and feel comfortable with from the thousands of plants available.

CLIMATE	PLANT	SOIL TYPE	SUGGESTED USES
WOOD • GREEN/BLUE			
COOL TEMPERATE/ CONTINENTAL (MINIMUM –20C TO 18C)	Festuca glauca Asplenium scolopendrium Eryngium amethystinum	Free-draining Alkaline or rich/moisture-retentive Alkaline or free-draining	For borders In shade For borders
TEMPERATE (MINIMUM –4C TO 18C)	Sinarundinaria nitida Hosta sieboldiana Meconopsis betonicifolia	Rich/moisture-retentive Rich/moisture-retentive Acid or rich/moisture-retentive	In shade, for height, for containers Ground cover, in shade, for containers In shade
WARM TEMPERATE/ MEDITERRANEAN (MINIMUM –1C TO 25C)	Pelargonium tomentosum Adiantum capillus-veneris Dicksonia antarctica	Free-draining Alkaline or rich/moisture-retentive Rich/moisture-retentive	For containers In shade In shade, for height
TROPICAL (MINIMUM 18C TO 30C)	Solanum wendlandii Strongylodon macrobotrys Neomarica caerulea	Free-draining Rich/moisture-retentive Rich/moisture-retentive	Climber, for height Climber Ground cover, in shade
FIRE • RED			
COOL TEMPERATE/ CONTINENTAL (MINIMUM –20C TO 18C)	Lychnis chalcedonica Lilium bulbiferum Vaccinium vitis-idaea	Free-draining Rich/moisture-retentive Acid or rich/moisture-retentive	For borders, for spot colour For containers, for spot colour Ground cover, in shade
TEMPERATE (MINIMUM –4C TO 18C)	Euphorbia griffithii Phygelius capensis Eucalyptus leucoxylon 'Rosea'	Free-draining Free-draining Free-draining	For borders For borders For height
WARM TEMPERATE/ MEDITERRANEAN (MINIMUM –1C TO 25C)	Lotus berthelotii Callistemon citrinus 'Splendens' Clivia miniata	Free-draining Free-draining Free-draining	Ground cover, for containers For borders In shade, for containers
TROPICAL (MINIMUM 18C TO 30C)	Passiflora coccinea Acalypha hispida Hibiscus rosa-sinensis	Rich/moisture-retentive Rich/moisture-retentive Rich/moisture-retentive	Climber For borders, for containers, for spot colour For borders, for containers, for spot colour

CLIMATE	PLANT	SOIL TYPE	SUGGESTED USES
EARTH • YELLOW/ORANGE			
COOL TEMPERATE/ CONTINENTAL (MINIMUM –20C TO 18C)	Solidago canadensis Rudbeckia fulgida Clematis tangutica	Free-draining Free-draining Alkaline	For borders For borders Climber, for height
TEMPERATE (MINIMUM –4C TO 18C)	Alstroemeria aurea Hemerocallis aurantiaca Hypericum calycinum	Free-draining Free-draining Free-draining	For borders, for spot colour For borders Ground cover, in shade
WARM TEMPERATE/ MEDITERRANEAN (MINIMUM –1C TO 25C)	Tecomaria capensis Solandra maxima Acacia dealbata	Free-draining Free-draining Acid	Climber, for height Climber, for height For height
TROPICAL (MINIMUM 18C TO 30C)	Allamanda cathartica Heliconia psittacorum Pyrostegia venusta	Rich/moisture-retentive Rich/moisture-retentive Free-draining	Climber Ground cover, in shade Climber, for height
METAL • WHITE/SILVER			
COOL TEMPERATE/ CONTINENTAL (MINIMUM –20C TO 18C)	Achillea ptarmica Betula papyrifera Tanacetum argentum	Rich/moisture-retentive Free-draining Alkaline or free-draining	For borders For height Ground cover
TEMPERATE (MINIMUM –4C TO 18C)	Artemisia absinthium Stachys byzantina Cistus laurifolius	Free-draining Free-draining Alkaline or free-draining	For borders Ground cover For borders
WARM TEMPERATE/ MEDITERRANEAN (MINIMUM –1C TO 25C)	Romneya coulteri Trachelospermum jasminoides Leptospermum scoparium	Free-draining Acid Acid or free-draining	Ground cover, for borders Climber, for height For borders
TROPICAL (MINIMUM 18C TO 30C)	Eucharis amazonica Jasminum sambac Coffea arabica	Rich/moisture-retentive Free-draining Rich/moisture-retentive	In shade, for borders, for containers Climber For borders, for containers
WATER • BLUE/BLACK			
COOL TEMPERATE/ CONTINENTAL (MINIMUM –20C TO 18C)	Aster ericoides Hyssopus officinalis Wisteria floribunda	Rich/moisture-retentive Alkaline Free-draining	For borders Ground cover Climber, for height
TEMPERATE (MINIMUM –4C TO 18C)	Geranium phaeum Gentiana asclepiadea Ophiopon planiscapus 'Nigrescens'	Free-draining Acid or rich/moisture-retentive Rich/moisture-retentive	In shade In shade In shade
WARM TEMPERATE/ MEDITERRANEAN (MINIMUM –1C TO 25C)	Plumbago auriculata Lavandula stoechas Agapanthus africanus	Free-draining Free-draining Free-draining	Climber For borders, for containers For containers
TROPICAL (MINIMUM 18C TO 30C)	Chamaedorea metallica Passiflora edulis Thunbergia grandiflora	Rich/moisture-retentive Rich/moisture-retentive Rich/moisture-retentive	In shade, for containers Climber, for height Climber, for height

The Eyes to See

We have seen throughout the book that how we place ourselves in our environment, and the images and symbols with which we surround ourselves, can have a profound effect on us psychologically. Our problems can be mirrored in our surroundings.

SYMBOLS AND IMAGES
~ Depression ~

Astrological systems indicate our high and low periods. If we recognize the signs, we can minimize the low ones. Just as injured animals take themselves off to a safe place, when we hurt we, too, hide away from the public view. Unless hurt, we would not willingly place ourselves behind a hedge such as that shown below left. There is no open view or *Ming Tang* in front of the house. Almost inevitably, the person who lives in this house will be depressed. A view of the sky places

us in our rightful place between heaven and earth. With the hedge reduced to the height of the window sill, the occupant will have a chance to connect with the world once again, and have a more objective view of his or her problems.

The spiked plant (*below right*) is more concerning. It would be impossible to sleep well in this room and its occupant would be fortunate indeed not to suffer from nightmares – imagine the noise against the window in the wind. This occupant will be nervous and highly strung and, again, living an insular life, though perhaps with a slightly unbalanced

ABOVE. *This tall hedge acts as a barrier between the occupant of the house and the outside world.*

RIGHT. *This spiked plant must surely disturb the person sleeping in this room and could indicate personal problems.*

view of the world. Imagine this bungalow with the plant removed, a clear path around it and a blue ceanothus and a cotoneaster, with its fiery red berries, to energize the Earth-shaped building, planted on the wall.

— Restriction —

There are times when we invent reasons to prevent us from moving on in our lives; again, it is possible to 'read' this frame of mind in a house. In the example shown below the ivy is restricting the window, not only by almost completely covering it but also by preventing maintenance, and it is unlikely that the window can be opened properly. Should the house require painting, the owner will probably keep postponing this task, since, before it can be done, a great deal of pruning will need to take place. It could be that until the house is painted it cannot be sold, and yet until the house

ABOVE. *These trees resemble bouncers. It will be a constant battle to get through the door. This factor, together with the sloping road, indicates that life is an uphill struggle.*

BELOW. *This ivy is not only preventing adequate maintenance of the window itself, but is also preventing the occupant from having a clear view of life.*

is sold the occupant will not be able to move away to a new job … and so the restriction continues.

The trees on either side of the door shown above are restricting in a different way. On a purely physical level, imagine squeezing between them with several shopping bags while searching for the door key! The narrow porch compounds the image. The trees will be menacing at night, and first thing in the morning it will seem quite a struggle just to leave the house. The view from the door will show the brown side of the trees which receive no natural light, and thus cannot be particularly pleasant. The occupant will feel unable to make changes in life and, since the road slopes, too, may regard life as a bit of an uphill struggle. To remove these trees, which have obviously been around for a while, will be a big hurdle to overcome. However, once this has been done, and the trees replaced with some pots of bright flowers, life's path will seem much easier.

CASE STUDY
Suburban Front Garden

A first glance at this house (*below*) suggests an eager-to-please executive, who works very hard but has never quite made it to the top. The dramatic red lead-up to this house tails off as it nears the entrance, as if the occupant arrives home at the end of the day, fired up or even angry, and then hides away from the world, shunning social contact until it is time to go to work again. Perhaps this person is never one of the 'in-crowd' but always at the beck and call of the boss, looking over their shoulder and expecting the worst. The overall feel is of petulant frustration and unrealized ambition, combined with underlying insecurity.

and there is a sulky feel to the house. The fiery planting is not restful to come home to, and there is too much of one colour and one season here.

A FENG SHUI REDESIGN
First, we need to address the house entrance. Solid steps facing the front indicate a more definite approach, and different colours raise the energy there. We need to move away from Earth colours, and a bright canopy

The entrance is now less oppressive. The black front door (Water) is correct for the white (Metal) and green (Wood) canopy. Tone down the white with terracotta pots (Earth) with red plants or berries (Fire) to complete the five-element cycle.

The steps appear to go two ways, indicating indecision, and the open treads signal insecurity. The shape and colour of the house is Earth, creating a depressing energy – as does the beam across the front of the house. The wall feature resembles a guillotine or axe about to fall, and the lamp-post halfway up the path leaves the driveway in darkness. Despite the length of the garden, the drawn curtains and large tree in front of the windows are restricting,

A solid staircase with a single entrance point removes the indecision at the entrance. The rounded steps and open area (*Ming Tang*) create a welcoming space.

Now the tree has been removed and the curtains drawn back, the occupant is offered a wider view and the possibility to follow his or her own vision.

would lighten the entrance area. Replacing the axe with an inspiring image and adding uplighters under the beam at either end alleviates the oppressive feel. Removing the tree offers a wider view of the world and will help the occupant put work problems into perspective. Moving the lamp-post to hide the corner of the building which shoots a 'poison arrow' at the drive makes the homecoming more welcoming and ensures that both path and driveway are lit.

Since most of the plants are in bloom at the same time, this garden must be dull for the rest of the year, particularly as there are no broad-leaved plants to maintain a balance. Cooler colours, and a lusher, greener planting, with an occasional architectural plant to lift the energy, would make this a more restful place. The red shrub on the corner outside the house is useful to add to the Fire element feeding the Earth shape.

This rising sun lifts the energy and indicates expansion and growth.

A green trim on a white facade utilizes more energetic colours and makes the house brighter.

Uplighters will raise the beam and, together with the red plant on the corner, will introduce the Fire element into the cycle.

The lamp-post moved to this corner hides the 'poison arrow' which pointed at the drive, and lights both path and drive.

The Water element is represented in the meandering planting.

The planting is cooler and less angry. Broad-leaved plants, together with the occasional architectural plant, raise the energy and create an overall balance.

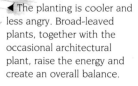

KEY		
∩	Wood element (*see page* 27)	
∧	Fire element (*see page* 28)	
⊓	Earth element (*see page* 29)	
∩	Metal element (*see page* 30)	
≈	Water element (*see page* 31)	

CASE STUDY
Balcony

From a Feng Shui perspective, the balcony below has to be one of the worst examples of a contemporary building. There is little balance or harmony and a magnificent view has been wrecked by a jumble of metal uprights and beams.

Beams are not favoured in Feng Shui since they can feel oppressive, although their effect in a barn with a vaulted roof is vastly different from that on a low cottage ceiling. Beams can also give an impression of cutting something in two, and those on this balcony certainly sit menacingly over the table.

REMEDIAL POSSIBILITIES

These are based on the principles of balance or concealment, dependent upon financial and structural considerations. The first two options are: to remove the overhead beams and the upright in the top right corner, structural constraints permitting;

or, if the beams cannot be removed, to instal a roof underneath to hide them from view. In both instances, the unbalanced window with its single upright is problematic. Often when a view is partially obscured problems can arise, physically and mentally, from blocked vision. Whatever our solution, we should aim to allow both eyes to observe the view from the same focal length. By establishing narrow panels on either side of the window we can balance the view and solve the problem.

The third – and easiest – option is to paint the beams white. This minimizes the oppressive feeling, and enables the beams to blend in with the sea and the sky, thus reducing their input.

ADDRESSING THE PROBLEMS

The difficulties created by this balcony are internal as well as external, and we should attempt to deal with them from inside the apartment. The beams have created two 'poison arrow' shadows. These should be blocked, as should the view of the beams. Natural views in the Phoenix position are important, and our aim should be to minimize the problems while maintaining as open a vista as possible. By using a light muslin drape above the window and a muslin panel on either side, we can balance the view and obscure the beams and the next-door balcony, while retaining light and most of the view of the sea and sky.

A small piece of furniture will block the 'poison arrows' and, with a plant on top, will serve to obscure the external upright. A large pot plant placed against the upright outside on the balcony will achieve the same purpose. Tall cordyline plants, or similar, will allow the light through and will also, because of their pointed leaves, add some Fire energy to balance the overwhelming Earth energy of the balcony.

We should aim not to sit or sunbathe directly under the beams, although the large umbrella covering the table and chairs helps reduce their impact. A minimalist approach to planting is appropriate here, and some red pelargoniums in front of the uprights will soften them while also preserving the view.

$\wedge$ Terracotta pots of red pelargoniums will hide the uprights and add some colour, again bringing the Fire element on to the balcony to improve the elemental balance.

White floaty muslin curtains will hide the beams from view inside the house, and will also hide the balcony next door.

Uprights and beams should be painted white to enable them to blend in with the background.

A tall plant will hide the external upright while letting light through and allowing a glimpse of the sea.

$\wedge$ A cordyline plant in a tall pot on the balcony will hide a fair proportion of the upright and will introduce the Fire element to the balcony.

$\cap$ Green would be a more restful colour for the railings and would introduce the Wood element to temper the overwhelming Earth energy and improve the balance.

A cabinet inside the window will cover the cross-beam and hide the 'poison arrows' created by the shadows of the beams.

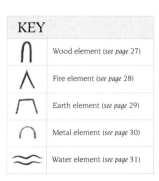

KEY	
$\cap$	Wood element (*see page 27*)
$\wedge$	Fire element (*see page 28*)
$\sqcap$	Earth element (*see page 29*)
$\cap$	Metal element (*see page 30*)
$\approx$	Water element (*see page 31*)

Kitchen Garden

This is a typical urban kitchen garden (*below*), with straight lines and formal planting. The length of the rows means the soil must be trodden on to weed and pull the crops, and this will compact it and damage the structure. The immaculate lawn, with its razor-sharp edges, and weed-free soil indicate a garden largely controlled by chemicals. The crops are grown in monocultural blocks, so when they are harvested the ground will be uncovered and may be eroded and open to weed seeds. This type of garden has seasonal interest only.

The large bush on the left must take moisture from beneath the crops and will need constant

attention to prevent it overshadowing them. The branch hanging over the fence at the end will create shade before long and, as it appears to be dying, could be removed. The post is not in proportion

with its position, and the lilac in the corner, though attractive now, will soon blend into the fence in this shady area and spend the rest of the year sending suckers into the vegetable patch. The shaded boundaries in the north and east are useful for utility areas and storage.

MAKING IMPROVEMENTS

First, we can remove the chore of lawn-edging by creating a path. The formality can be retained for easy maintenance while introducing a more informal feel with the planting. We can apply permaculture design principles to take account of the direction and weather, our movement through the plot and the supportive network of planting. The aim is to create some winter interest, and to incorporate the five-element principles so obviously lacking. We can also make the kitchen plot an integral part of the garden.

Water-butts can collect the water from the shed roof.

⌒ A Metal-shaped arch with an open Tai Chi area will allow the chi to circulate and can be covered by yellow climbing roses, tied well in to prevent them from obstructing the pathways.

With the lilac removed, this area may be used for compost – a useful place since it is the Wealth area.

A statue or pedestal with an urn here will draw the vegetable plot into the garden design.

Since this area is shady, a *Clematis montana* here, pink for the Relationships area, would raise the energy and eventually grow right along the fence and through the trees, again drawing the kitchen plot into the garden.

● Since the garden faces south we can use the Tortoise, Dragon and Tiger formation to surround three sides of the plot. This will give the garden some height and allow us to grow espalier fruit and climbing plants, beans, nasturtiums, sweet peas and gourds. The trellis will filter the wind and shield the utility areas from view.

∧ Wigwams for runner beans can be dotted here and there to introduce the Fire element.

◄ Jerusalem artichokes, fruit bushes and rhubarb can hug the periphery and provide protection for the smaller plants in front. Since the garden faces south we need to keep the side planting on the west lower than that on the east to provide more access to evening light – the Tiger should give way to the Dragon.

Although the garden is formal in design, we can introduce keyhole beds to allow easy access to all parts of the plot. The edges of the raised beds should be cropped to save ankles from brushing against the plants and to create turning room for a wheelbarrow.

▲ A mixed planting of herbs and vegetables allows planting times to be staggered to provide a year-round selection of vegetables, as well as companion support.

KEY		
∩	Wood element (*see page* 27)	
∧	Fire element (*see page* 28)	
⊓	Earth element (*see page* 29)	
∩	Metal element (*see page* 30)	
〰	Water element (*see page* 31)	

✑ MOON AND COMPANION PLANTING ✑

The following information allows us to offer our plants optimum conditions in time and place. Plants may thrive alongside some plants yet become distressed near others. Planting in the best moon phase can greatly influence a plant's growth, and certain constellations can enhance special plant properties. We can also use these techniques to harvest crops and perform garden tasks. (NOTE: Where no companion plants are listed, there is no available research. As you experiment in the garden, try adding to the table yourself.) The moon phase and constellation can be determined by consulting the sky, a moon chart, planting tables or an ephemeris (*see page* 125).

PLANT	COMPANION: YES	COMPANION: NO	PHASE	SIGN
ANGELICA	Parsley	Celery	1	Cancer Scorpio Pisces
ANISE	Cabbage, Coriander		1–2	Capricorn
ANNUALS			1–2	
APPLE	Blackberry, Chives, Foxgloves, Garlic, Mint, Nasturtiums, Sage, Tansies	Carrots, Potatoes	3	Cancer Virgo Pisces
APRICOT	Basil, Nasturtiums, Tansies	Potatoes, Southernwood, Tomatoes,	3	Taurus Virgo Libra
ARTICHOKE: *Globe*	Parsley	Garlic	3	Libra Cancer Pisces
Jerusalem	Sweetcorn		3	Taurus Virgo Capricorn
ASPARAGUS	Basil, Grapes, Marigolds, Parsley, Tomatoes	Chives, Garlic, Leeks, Onions	3	Cancer Scorpio Pisces
ASPARAGUS PEA	Camomile		2	Cancer Scorpio Pisces
AUBERGINE	Beans, Peas, Potatoes, Tarragon, Thyme	Garlic, Onions	2	Cancer Libra Scorpio Pisces
BASIL	Apricot, Asparagus, Grapes, Marigolds, Parsley, Summer Savory, Tomatoes	Rue, Tansy, Wormwood	1–2	Cancer Scorpio Pisces
BAY	Grapes		3	Taurus Scorpio Pisces
BEANS: *All*	Beetroot, Borage, Brassicas, Carrots, Cauliflower, Cucumber, Marigolds, Petunias, Tomatoes, Strawberries, Summer Savory, Sweetcorn	Chives, Garlic, Kohlrabi, Leeks, Onion, Sunflowers	2	Taurus Cancer Libra Scorpio Pisces
Broad	Chervil, Gooseberry, Marjoram, Peas, Potatoes, Rosemary, Spinach, Thyme, Winter Savory	Fennel, Horseradish, Nasturtiums	2	Taurus Cancer Libra Scorpio Pisces
Dwarf	Asparagus, Celery, Marjoram, Potatoes, Rosemary, Soya beans, Squash, Thyme	Fennel, Horseradish	2	Taurus Cancer Libra Scorpio Pisces
Runner	Aubergines, Celeriac, Marjoram, Peas, Radish, Rosemary, Sweet Peas, Winter Savory	Beetroot, Broccoli, Brassicas, Cauliflower, Horseradish, Nasturtiums, Strawberries, Sunflowers, Swede	2	Taurus Cancer Libra Scorpio Pisces
Soya	Dwarf beans, Strawberries	Chives, Garlic, Leeks, Onions	2	Cancer Scorpio Pisces Libra
BEECH		Ferns	3	Cancer Scorpio Pisces
BEETROOT	Broad beans, French beans, Brassicas, Chervil, Cucumber, Dill, Garlic, Kohlrabi, Lettuce, Onions	Runner beans, Tomatoes	3	Cancer Libra Scorpio Capricorn Pisces
BERGAMOT	Brassicas, Mint, Parsley		1	Cancer Libra Scorpio Pisces
BERRIES			2	Cancer Scorpio Pisces

PLANT	COMPANION: YES	COMPANION: NO	PHASE	SIGN
BLACKBERRIES	Apples, Tansies		2	Cancer Scorpio Pisces
BLACKCURRANTS	Wormwood		2	Cancer Scorpio Pisces
BORAGE	Broad beans, Courgettes, Cucumber, Marrow, Squash, Strawberries, Tomatoes		1	Libra
BROCCOLI	Camomile, Caraway, Celeriac, Celery, Dill, Hyssop, Kohlrabi, Mint, Potatoes, Rosemary, Sage, Southernwood, Thyme, Wormwood	Runner beans, Lettuce, Summer Spinach, Strawberries, Winter Tomatoes	1	Taurus Cancer Scorpio
BRUSSELS SPROUTS	Camomile, Caraway, Celeriac, Celery, Dill, Hyssop, Mint, Oregano, Potatoes, Rosemary, Sage, Thyme, Southernwood, Sweetcorn, Wormwood	Runner beans, Onions, Radishes, Spinach, Tomatoes, Vines	1	Taurus Cancer Scorpio Pisces
BULBS			3	Cancer Virgo Libra Scorpio Pisces
CABBAGE	Asparagus, Beetroot, Bergamot, Broad beans, Camomile, Celeriac, Celery, Chervil, Chick Peas, Chives, Dill, Dwarf beans, Fennel, Horseradish, Hyssop, Lavender, Marjoram, Mint, Nasturtiums, Oregano, Peas, Pennyroyal Potatoes, Pumpkin, Rosemary, Sage, Southernwood, Thyme, Wormwood	Garlic, Grapes, Lettuce, Onions, Radishes, Rue, Runner beans, Spinach, Strawberries, Tomatoes	1	Cancer Scorpio Pisces
CAMOMILE	Brassicas (Broccoli, Cauliflower), Kohlrabi, Mint, Onions, Peas, Potatoes	Rue	1	Cancer Libra Scorpio Pisces
CARAWAY	Brussels Sprouts, Cauliflower, Kohlrabi, Peas	Fennel, Tomatoes	1	Capricorn
CARROTS	Broad beans, Celeriac, Celery, Chives, Coriander, Cucumber, Garlic, Leeks, Lettuce, Onions, Parsnips, Peas, Radishes, Rosemary, Sage, Salsify, Spinach, Tomatoes, Wormwood	Anise, Dill	3	Taurus Cancer Scorpio Pisces
CATMINT	Radishes, Southernwood, Strawberries, Swede, Thyme, Turnips		3	Libra Scorpio
CAULIFLOWER	Broad beans, Caraway, Celeriac, Celery, Dill, Hyssop, Mint, Potatoes, Rosemary, Sage, Southernwood, Thyme, Wormwood	Beetroot, Radishes, Spinach, Strawberries, Tomatoes	1	Cancer Scorpio Pisces
CELERIAC	Brassicas, Carrots, Onions, Runner beans, Tomatoes		3	Taurus Cancer Libra Scorpio Pisces
CELERY	Broccoli, Brassicas, Chervil, Cauliflower, Dill, Dwarf beans, Garlic, Kohlrabi, Leeks, Lettuce, Runner beans, Tomatoes	Angelica, Lovage	1	Cancer Scorpio Pisces
CEREALS			1–2	Cancer Libra Scorpio Pisces
CHERRY		Plum	2–3	Taurus Virgo Libra
CHERVIL	Beetroot, Broad beans, Cabbage, Camomile, Garlic, Lettuce, Onions, Radishes	Rue	1	Cancer Scorpio Pisces
CHICORY			2–3	Cancer Scorpio Pisces
CHINESE GREENS			1	Cancer Scorpio Pisces
CHIVES	Apple, Cabbage, Carrots, Chrysanthemums, Cucumber, Currants, Gooseberries, Grapes, Leeks, Peaches, Roses, Sunflowers, Tomatoes	Asparagus, Broad beans, Marjoram, Peas, Runner beans, Soya beans	2–3	Sagittarius

PLANT	COMPANION: YES	COMPANION: NO	PHASE	SIGN
CLIMBERS			1–2	*Leaves and Flowers:* Gemini Virgo Libra *Fruit:* Cancer Scorpio Pisces
CLOVES	Strawberries		1	Capricorn
COMFREY	Potatoes, Tomatoes		3	Cancer Virgo Pisces
CORIANDER	Anise, Radishes, Spinach	Fennel	1	Cancer Scorpio Pisces
CORMS			3	Cancer Virgo Libra Scorpio Pisces
COURGETTES	Basil, Beans, Borage, Fennel, Nasturtiums, Peas, Sweetcorn, Tansies	Potatoes, Rosemary, Rue, Sage, Thyme	2	Cancer Libra Scorpio Pisces
CUCUMBER	Borage, Broad beans, Cabbage, Carrots, Celery, Dill, Dwarf beans, Horseradish, Kohlrabi, Lettuce, Lovage, Nasturtiums, Onions, Parsley, Pear, Peas, Radishes, Sunflowers, Sweetcorn, Tansies, Yarrow	Marjoram, Potatoes, Sage, Thyme	1	Cancer Scorpio Pisces
CURRANTS			2	Cancer Scorpio Pisces
DILL	Brassicas (Broccoli, Cauliflower), Cabbage, Celery, Cucumber, Kohlrabi Leeks, Lettuce, Onions, Radishes, Spinach, Sweetcorn, Tomatoes	Carrots, Fennel	1	Cancer Scorpio Pisces
ENDIVE			1	Cancer Scorpio Pisces
FENNEL	Cabbage, Courgettes, Herbs, Leeks, Marrows, Squashes	Basil, Broad beans, Caraway, Coriander, Dwarf beans, Horehound, Kohlrabi, Lemon Balm, Lettuce, Rue, Tarragon, Tomatoes, Turnips, Wormwood	1	Cancer Scorpio Pisces
FLOWERS: *Annuals*			1	Virgo Libra
Biennials			3	Virgo Libra
Perennials			3	Virgo Libra
GARLIC	Apples, Beetroot, Blackberries, Carrots, Chervil, Currants, Gooseberries, Lettuce, Onions, Peaches, Pears, Plums, Roses, Raspberries, Rhubarb, Strawberries	Artichokes, Asparagus, Aubergines, Beans, Cabbage, Marjoram, Peas, Soya Beans	1–2	Scorpio Sagittarius
GOOSEBERRIES	Broad beans, Currants, Garlic, Tansies, Tomatoes		2	Cancer Scorpio Pisces
GOURDS			1–2	Cancer Scorpio Pisces
GRAPES	Asparagus, Basil, Blackberries, Borage, Elm, Hyssop, Mulberries, Sage, Tansies	Cabbage, Radishes, Sage	1–2	Cancer Scorpio Pisces
GRASS			1–2	Cancer Scorpio Pisces
HONEYSUCKLE			2	Virgo Scorpio
HOPS			2	Scorpio
HORSERADISH	Apples, Cabbage, Cucumber, Plums, Potatoes, Spinach, Thyme	Beans, Peas	3	Cancer Scorpio
HYSSOP	Brassicas (Broccoli, Cauliflower), Grapes, Horehound, Kohlrabi	Radishes	3	Cancer Scorpio Pisces

PLANT	COMPANION: YES	COMPANION: NO	PHASE	SIGN
KOHLRABI	Beetroot, Borage, Broad beans, Camomile, Caraway, Celery, Cucumber, Dill, Hyssop, Mint, Onions, Potatoes, Rosemary, Sage, Southernwood, Thyme, Wormwood	Dwarf beans, Fennel, Peppers, Runner beans, Spinach, Strawberries Tomatoes	1	Cancer Libra Scorpio Pisces
LAVENDER	Cabbage, Marjoram, Potatoes, Thyme	Lettuce, Parsley, Rue	3	Cancer Libra Pisces
LEEKS	Carrots, Celeriac, Celery, Chives, Dill, Fennel, Onions, Strawberries	Asparagus, Beans, Broccoli, Marjoram, Peas, Soya Beans	2–3	Sagittarius
LEMON BALM	Most plants	Fennel, Rue	1	Cancer Scorpio Pisces
LETTUCE	Basil, Beans, Beetroot, Carrots, Chervil, Cucumber, Currants, Dill, Garlic, Leeks, Onions, Parsley, Peas, Radishes, Strawberries, Thyme, Tomatoes	Broccoli, Fennel, Lavender, Rue	1	Cancer Libra Scorpio Pisces
LOGANBERRIES			2	Cancer Scorpio Pisces
LOVAGE	Cucumber, Parsnips	Celery	1	Cancer Scorpio Pisces
MARIGOLDS	Asparagus, Basil, Beans, Cabbage, Peas, Potatoes, Roses, Tomatoes		2	Libra
MARJORAM	Beans, Cabbage, Lavender, Potatoes	Cucumber, Garlic, Leeks, Onions	1	Cancer Scorpio Pisces
MARROWS	Borage, Fennel, Nasturtiums, Sweetcorn	Potatoes, Sage, Thyme	2	Cancer Libra Scorpio Pisces
MELON	Potatoes		2	Cancer Scorpio Pisces
MINT	Apple, Bergamot, Broccoli, Brussels Sprouts, Cauliflower, Kohlrabi, Peas, Pears, Potatoes, Tomatoes, Walnuts		1	Cancer Scorpio Pisces
MULBERRIES	Grapes		3	Taurus Cancer Virgo Pisces
NASTURTIUMS	Apples, Broccoli, Cabbage, Courgettes, Cucumbers, Marrow, Pears, Potatoes, Pumpkin, Radishes, Squashes, Tomatoes	Broad beans	2	Cancer Virgo Libra Pisces
ONIONS	Beetroot, Brassicas (Kohlrabi), Camomile, Carrots, Celeriac, Cloves, Cucumber, Dill, Leeks, Lettuce, Parsley, Parsnips, Strawberries, Summer Savory, Thyme, Tomatoes	Asparagus, Aubergines, Beans, Marjoram, Peas, Soya Beans	Seeds: 2 Sets: 3	Seeds: Scorpio Sagittarius Sets: Taurus Libra Pisces
OREGANO	Brassicas		1	Cancer Scorpio Pisces
PARSLEY	Angelica, Artichokes, Asparagus, Basil, Bergamot, Lovage, Potatoes, Tomatoes	Cabbage, Lavender, Lettuce	1	Cancer Libra Scorpio Pisces
PARSNIPS	Lettuce, Onions, Peas	Peppers	3	Cancer Libra Scorpio Pisces
PEACHES	Garlic		2–3	Taurus Virgo Libra
PEAS	Aubergines, Beans, Carrots, Celeriac, Celery, Cucumber, Lettuce, Marigolds, Mint, Potatoes, Radishes, Swedes, Sweetcorn, Turnips	Garlic, Horseradish, Leeks, Onions	2	Cancer Libra Scorpio Pisces
PEARS	Cucumber, Garlic, Mint, Nasturtiums, Spinach, Sweetcorn, Tansies		2–3	Taurus Virgo Libra
PENNYROYAL	Broccoli, Brussels Sprouts, Cabbage	Kohlrabi, Parsnips	2–3	Taurus Virgo Libra
PEPPERS: *Sweet*	Aubergine, Basil	Brassicas, Grapes, Hyssop	2	Scorpio Sagittarius
Chilli	Chervil, Mustard, Nasturtiums		2	Scorpio Sagittarius

PLANT	COMPANION: YES	COMPANION: NO	PHASE	SIGN
PERENNIALS			3	
PLUMS	Currants, Garlic, Raspberries	Chervil	2–3	Taurus Virgo Libra
POTATOES	Aubergines, Beans, Brassicas (Broccoli, Cauliflower, Kohlrabi), Celery, Dill, Foxgloves, Horseradish, Lamium, Lavender, Lemon Balm, Marigolds, Mint, Nasturtiums, Parsley, Peas, Spinach, Strawberries, Summer Savory, Sweetcorn, Tagetes, Tarragon, Valerian	Apples, Apricots, Courgettes, Cucumber, Marrow, Onions, Orache, Pumpkins, Raspberries, Squashes, Sunflowers, Tomatoes	3	Taurus Cancer Libra Scorpio
PUMPKINS	Nasturtiums, Radishes, Tansies, Sweetcorn	Potatoes, Rosemary, Sage, Thyme	2	Cancer Libra Scorpio Pisces
RADISHES	Carrots, Catmint, Chervil, Chives, Coriander, Cucumber, Dill, Lettuce, Nasturtiums, Peas, Turnips	Brassicas (Cauliflower), Grapes, Hyssop, Summer Savory, Winter Savory	3	Taurus Libra Capricorn Pisces
RASPBERRIES	Garlic, Marigolds, Plums, Rue, Yarrow	Potatoes	1	Cancer Scorpio Pisces
RHUBARB	Brassicas, Garlic, Spinach		3	Cancer Scorpio Pisces
RICE			1–2	Scorpio
ROSEMARY	Beans, Broccoli, Carrots, Cauliflower, Kohlrabi, Sage, Tomatoes, Yarrow	Courgettes, Cucumber, Pumpkin, Squashes	3	Cancer Virgo Scorpio
ROSES	Chives, Garlic, Geraniums, Marigolds, Parsley, Rue, Tansies, Thyme, Tomatoes		1–2	Cancer
RUE	Figs, Raspberries, Roses	Basil, Camomile, Chervil, Courgettes, Lavender, Lemon Balm, Lettuce, Sage, Tarragon, Yarrow	1	Cancer Virgo Pisces
SAGE	Brassicas (Broccoli, Cauliflower), Carrots, Kohlrabi, Tomatoes	Courgettes, Cucumber, Pumpkins, Rosemary, Rue, Squashes, Wormwood	1	Cancer Scorpio Pisces
SHALLOTS			Seeds: 2 Sets: 3–4	Scorpio Sagittarius
SORRELL			1	Cancer Scorpio Pisces
SOUTHERNWOOD	Apricots, Brassicas (Broccoli, Cauliflower, Kohlrabi), Catmint		1	Cancer Pisces
SPINACH	Broad beans, Coriander, Dill, Horseradish, Pear, Rhubarb, Strawberries, Sweetcorn	Brassicas (Broccoli, Cauliflower, Kohlrabi), Radishes	1	Cancer Scorpio Pisces
SPRING ONIONS			2	Scorpio Sagittarius
SQUASHES	Borage, Dwarf beans, Fennel, Nasturtiums, Potatoes, Sweetcorn	Rosemary, Sage, Thyme	2	Cancer Scorpio Pisces
STRAWBERRIES	Borage, Dwarf beans, Endive, Leeks, Lettuce, Onion, Soya beans, Spinach, Tansies	Brassicas (Broccoli, Cauliflower, Kohlrabi), Garlic	3	Cancer Scorpio Pisces
SUMMER SAVORY	Basil, Beans, Onions	Radishes, Turnips	1	Cancer Scorpio Pisces
SUNFLOWERS	Cucumber, Sweetcorn	Beetroot, Brassicas (Broccoli), Potatoes, Runner beans	3	Libra Capricorn
SWEDE	Catmint, Peas, Pears		3	Taurus
SWEETCORN	Beans, Brussels Sprouts, Courgettes, Cucumber, Dill, Marrows, Peas, Pears, Potatoes, Pumpkins, Spinach, Squashes, Yarrow		1	Cancer Scorpio Pisces

PLANT	COMPANION: YES	COMPANION: NO	PHASE	SIGN
TANSIES	Apples, Apricots, Blackberries, Courgettes, Cucumber, Gooseberries, Grapes, Pears, Pumpkins, Roses, Strawberries	Basil	1	Cancer Scorpio Pisces
TARRAGON	Aubergines, Potatoes	Fennel, Rue	1	Cancer Scorpio Pisces
THYME	Most plants	Courgettes, Cucumber, Pumpkin, Squashes	1	Cancer Scorpio Pisces
TOMATOES	Asparagus, Basil, Borage, Carrots, Celeriac, Celery, Chives, Dill, Dwarf beans, Gooseberries, Horseradish, Lemon Balm, Marigolds, Mint, Nasturtiums, Onions, Parsley, Roses, Rosemary, Sage, Spinach, Thyme	Apricots, Brassicas (Broccoli, Cauliflower, Kohlrabi), Caraway, Fennel, Potatoes, Wormwood	2	Cancer Pisces Scorpio
TREES: Deciduous			3	Cancer Virgo Scorpio Pisces
Evergreen			3	Taurus Cancer Virgo Scorpio Pisces
Nut			1	Taurus
TURNIPS	Catmint, Peas, Radishes, Thyme	Fennel, Summer Savory, Wormwood	3	Taurus Cancer Libra Scorpio Capricorn Pisces
VINES		Laurel	2	Foliage: Virgo Fruit: Cancer Libra Pisces
WINTER SAVORY	Beans	Radishes, Turnips	1	Cancer Scorpio Pisces
WORMWOOD	Brassicas (Broccoli, Cauliflower), Carrots	Basil, Caraway, Fennel, Sage, Tomatoes	1	Cancer Scorpio Pisces
YARROW	Rosemary	Rue	1	Cancer Scorpio Pisces

HARVESTING

PLANT		PHASE	SIGN
BEANS:	For now	2	Cancer Scorpio Pisces
	For storing	3–4	Aries Leo Sagittarius
FLOWERS		1–2	Gemini Virgo Libra
FRUIT:	For now	2	Cancer Scorpio Pisces
	For storing	3–4	Cancer Scorpio Pisces
HERBS:	Leaves (for now)	1–2	Cancer Scorpio Pisces
	Leaves (for storing)	3–4	Cancer Scorpio Pisces
	Seeds (for now)	2	Aries Leo Sagittarius
	Seeds (for storing)	3–4	Aries Leo Sagittarius
ONION FAMILY		3	Aries Leo Sagittarius
VEGETABLES:	Leaf Crops (for now)	1–2	Cancer Scorpio Pisces
	Leaf Crops (for storing)	3–4	Cancer Scorpio Pisces
	Roots (for now)	3	Taurus Virgo Capricorn
	Roots (for storing)	3–4	Taurus Virgo Capricorn

NOTE: Commonly grown crops and general garden tasks are listed here. If there are other crops or tasks particular to your garden, refer to the box on page 43 to help you judge which moon phase is most suitable.

GARDEN MAINTENANCE

TASK		PHASE	SIGN
COMPOST:	Make	4	Cancer Scorpio Pisces
	Spread	3–4	Cancer Scorpio Pisces
CUTTTING WOOD		4	Leo
FENCING		3–4	Taurus Leo
FERTILIZING		3–4	Taurus Cancer Scorpio Capricorn Pisces
MOWING GRASS:	New		Cancer Scorpio Pisces
	Established	3–4	Leo Virgo Sagittarius
MULCHING		3–4	Cancer Scorpio Pisces
PERENNIALS:	Divide in autumn	1	Cancer Scorpio Pisces
PRUNING:	To increase growth	1	Cancer Scorpio Pisces
	To maintain shape	3–4	Aries Gemini Leo Sagittarius Aquarius
SPRAYING		4	Aries Gemini Leo Sagittarius Aquarius
TRANSPLANTING		1–2	Cancer Scorpio Pisces
WATERING		1–2	Cancer Scorpio Pisces
WEEDING		3–4	Aries Gemini Leo Sagittarius Aquarius

ANIMALS, ELEMENTS AND YEAR DATES

This table includes the Chinese year dates and corresponding animal signs for the years 1924–2007. Each animal is associated with an Earthly Branch and its relative element which denotes its intrinsic nature. In every year of the sixty-year cycle (*see page* 55), each Earthly Branch connects with a Heavenly Stem which brings its own elemental quality denoting an animal or person's character.

Use the table to find out which animal and elements reflect your nature and character according to your year of birth (check the date on which the year begins – you may belong to the previous year). You can use these elements to focus on a particular area of the body (*see page* 25). The solar year dates are also included below so that you can calculate your personal element and direction (*see page* 39).

YEAR	CHINESE YEAR DATES	ANIMAL / EARTHLY BRANCH	HEAVENLY STEM	SOLAR YEAR BEGINS	YEAR	CHINESE YEAR DATES	ANIMAL / EARTHLY BRANCH	HEAVENLY STEM	SOLAR YEAR BEGINS
1924	5 Feb – 23 Jan 1925	Rat • Water	Wood	5 Feb	1966	21 Jan – 8 Feb 1967	Horse • Fire	Fire	4 Feb
1925	24 Jan – 12 Feb 1926	Ox • Earth	Wood	4 Feb	1967	9 Feb – 29 Jan 1968	Sheep • Earth	Fire	4 Feb
1926	13 Feb – 1 Feb 1927	Tiger • Wood	Fire	4 Feb	1968	30 Jan – 16 Feb 1969	Monkey • Metal	Earth	5 Feb
1927	2 Feb – 22 Jan 1928	Rabbit • Wood	Fire	5 Feb	1969	17 Feb – 5 Feb 1970	Rooster • Metal	Earth	4 Feb
1928	23 Jan – 9 Feb 1929	Dragon • Earth	Earth	5 Feb	1970	6 Feb – 26 Jan 1971	Dog • Earth	Metal	4 Feb
1929	10 Feb – 29 Jan 1930	Snake • Fire	Earth	4 Feb	1971	27 Jan – 15 Feb 1972	Pig • Water	Metal	4 Feb
1930	30 Jan – 16 Feb 1931	Horse • Fire	Metal	4 Feb	1972	16 Feb – 2 Feb 1973	Rat • Water	Water	5 Feb
1931	17 Feb – 5 Feb 1932	Sheep • Earth	Metal	5 Feb	1973	3 Feb – 22 Jan 1974	Ox • Earth	Water	4 Feb
1932	6 Feb – 25 Jan 1933	Monkey • Metal	Water	5 Feb	1974	23 Jan – 10 Feb 1975	Tiger • Wood	Wood	4 Feb
1933	26 Jan – 13 Feb 1934	Rooster • Metal	Water	4 Feb	1975	11 Feb – 30 Jan 1976	Rabbit • Wood	Wood	4 Feb
1934	14 Feb – 3 Feb 1935	Dog • Earth	Wood	4 Feb	1976	31 Jan – 17 Feb 1977	Dragon • Earth	Fire	5 Feb
1935	4 Feb – 23 Jan 1936	Pig • Water	Wood	5 Feb	1977	18 Feb – 6 Feb 1978	Snake • Fire	Fire	4 Feb
1936	24 Jan – 10 Feb 1937	Rat • Water	Fire	5 Feb	1978	7 Feb – 27 Jan 1979	Horse • Fire	Earth	4 Feb
1937	11 Feb – 30 Jan 1938	Ox • Earth	Fire	4 Feb	1979	28 Jan – 15 Feb 1980	Sheep • Earth	Earth	4 Feb
1938	31 Jan – 18 Feb 1939	Tiger • Wood	Earth	4 Feb	1980	16 Feb – 4 Feb 1981	Monkey • Metal	Metal	5 Feb
1939	19 Feb – 7 Feb 1940	Rabbit • Wood	Earth	5 Feb	1981	5 Feb – 24 Jan 1982	Rooster • Metal	Metal	4 Feb
1940	8 Feb – 26 Jan 1941	Dragon • Earth	Metal	5 Feb	1982	25 Jan – 12 Feb 1983	Dog • Earth	Water	4 Feb
1941	27 Jan – 14 Feb 1942	Snake • Fire	Metal	4 Feb	1983	13 Feb – 1 Feb 1984	Pig • Water	Water	4 Feb
1942	15 Feb – 4 Feb 1943	Horse • Fire	Water	4 Feb	1984	2 Feb – 19 Feb 1985	Rat • Water	Wood	4 Feb
1943	5 Feb – 24 Jan 1944	Sheep • Earth	Water	5 Feb	1985	20 Feb – 8 Feb 1986	Ox • Earth	Wood	4 Feb
1944	25 Jan – 12 Feb 1945	Monkey • Metal	Wood	5 Feb	1986	9 Feb – 28 Jan 1987	Tiger • Wood	Fire	4 Feb
1945	13 Feb – 1 Feb 1946	Rooster • Metal	Wood	4 Feb	1987	29 Jan – 16 Feb 1988	Rabbit • Wood	Fire	4 Feb
1946	2 Feb – 21 Jan 1947	Dog • Earth	Fire	4 Feb	1988	17 Feb – 5 Feb 1989	Dragon • Earth	Earth	4 Feb
1947	22 Jan – 9 Feb 1948	Pig • Water	Fire	4 Feb	1989	6 Feb – 26 Jan 1990	Snake • Fire	Earth	4 Feb
1948	10 Feb – 28 Jan 1949	Rat • Water	Earth	5 Feb	1990	27 Jan – 14 Feb 1991	Horse • Fire	Metal	4 Feb
1949	29 Jan – 16 Feb 1950	Ox • Earth	Earth	4 Feb	1991	15 Feb – 3 Feb 1992	Sheep • Earth	Metal	4 Feb
1950	17 Feb – 5 Feb 1951	Tiger • Wood	Metal	4 Feb	1992	4 Feb – 22 Jan 1993	Monkey • Metal	Water	4 Feb
1951	6 Feb – 26 Jan 1952	Rabbit • Wood	Metal	4 Feb	1993	23 Jan – 9 Feb 1994	Rooster • Metal	Water	4 Feb
1952	27 Jan – 13 Feb 1953	Dragon • Earth	Water	5 Feb	1994	10 Feb – 30 Jan 1995	Dog • Earth	Wood	4 Feb
1953	14 Feb – 2 Feb 1954	Snake • Fire	Water	4 Feb	1995	31 Jan – 18 Feb 1996	Pig • Water	Wood	4 Feb
1954	3 Feb – 23 Jan 1955	Horse • Fire	Wood	4 Feb	1996	19 Feb – 6 Feb 1997	Rat • Water	Fire	4 Feb
1955	24 Jan – 11 Feb 1956	Sheep • Earth	Wood	4 Feb	1997	7 Feb – 27 Jan 1998	Ox • Earth	Fire	4 Feb
1956	12 Feb – 30 Jan 1957	Monkey • Metal	Fire	5 Feb	1998	28 Jan – 15 Feb 1999	Tiger • Wood	Earth	4 Feb
1957	31 Jan – 17 Feb 1958	Rooster • Metal	Fire	4 Feb	1999	16 Feb – 4 Feb 2000	Rabbit • Wood	Earth	4 Feb
1958	18 Feb – 7 Feb 1959	Dog • Earth	Earth	4 Feb	2000	5 Feb – 23 Jan 2001	Dragon • Earth	Metal	4 Feb
1959	8 Feb – 27 Jan 1960	Pig • Water	Earth	4 Feb	2001	24 Jan – 11 Feb 2002	Snake • Fire	Metal	4 Feb
1960	28 Jan – 14 Feb 1961	Rat • Water	Metal	5 Feb	2002	12 Feb – 31 Jan 2003	Horse • Fire	Water	4 Feb
1961	15 Feb – 4 Feb 1962	Ox • Earth	Metal	4 Feb	2003	1 Feb – 21 Jan 2004	Sheep • Earth	Water	4 Feb
1962	5 Feb – 24 Jan 1963	Tiger • Wood	Water	4 Feb	2004	22 Jan – 8 Feb 2005	Monkey • Metal	Wood	4 Feb
1963	25 Jan – 12 Feb 1964	Rabbit • Wood	Water	4 Feb	2005	9 Feb – 28 Jan 2006	Rooster • Metal	Wood	4 Feb
1964	13 Feb – 1 Feb 1965	Dragon • Earth	Wood	5 Feb	2006	29 Jan – 17 Feb 2007	Dog • Earth	Fire	4 Feb
1965	2 Feb – 20 Jan 1966	Snake • Fire	Wood	4 Feb	2007	18 Feb – 6 Feb 2008	Pig • Water	Fire	4 Feb

Useful Addresses

BIODYNAMICS

United Kingdom

The Biodynamic Agricultural Association
Rudolf Steiner House
35 Park Road
London
NW1 6XT
Tel: (01562) 884933

Ireland

Biodynamic Association of Ireland
Ballinroan House
Kiltegan
Co. Wicklow

Australia

Biodynamic Gardeners Association
15 Dianne Street
Doncaster East
VIC 3109
Tel: (03) 9842 8137

ORGANIC AND ENVIRONMENTAL GROUPS

United Kingdom

Henry Doubleday Research Association (HYDRA)
National Centre for Organic Gardening
Ryton-on-Dunsmore
Coventry
CV8 3LG
Tel: (01203) 303517

The Soil Association
Bristol House
90 Victoria Street
Bristol
BS1 6DF
Tel: (0117) 929 0661
Fax: (0117) 925 2504

PERMACULTURE

United Kingdom

The Permaculture Association
PO Box 1
Buckfastleigh
Devon
TQ11 OLH
Tel: (01654) 712188

Australia

Permaculture Institute
South Pumpenbil Street
Tyalgum NSW
NSW 2484
Tel: (066) 79 3442

FENG SHUI

United Kingdom

Feng Shui Association
31 Woburn Place
Brighton
BN1 9GA
Tel/Fax: (01273) 693 844
E-mail: fengshui@mistral.co.uk

Feng Shui Society
PO Box 83
Camberley
Surrey
GU15 1XE
Tel: (07050) 289 200
Fax: (0171) 426 0931
E-mail: kayers@netcomuk.co.uk

Feng Shui Network International
PO Box 9
Pateley Bridge
Harrogate
HG3 5XG
Tel: (01423) 712868
Fax: (01423) 712869

School of Feng Shui
34 Banbury Road
Ettington
Stratford-upon-Avon
Warwickshire
CV37 7SU
Tel: (0178) 974 0116

Australia

Feng Shui Society of Australia
PO Box 6416
Shopping World
NSW 2060

Bibliography and Further Reading

GARDENING
Findhorn Community, *The Findhorn Garden: Pioneering a New Vision of Humanity and Nature in Cooperation*. Forres, Scotland: Findhorn Press, 1989 (2nd ed.).

Harper, Peter, *The Natural Garden Book: Gardening in Harmony with Nature*. London: Gaia Books Limited, 1994.

Minter, Sue, *The Healing Garden: A Natural Haven for Emotional and Physical Well-being*. London: Headline, 1993.

Thacker, Christopher, *The History of Gardens*. London: Croom Helm, 1979.

COMPANION PLANTING
Flowerdew, Bob, *Complete Book of Companion Planting*. London: Kyle Kathie Limited, 1993.

Franck, Gertrud, *Companion Planting: Successful Gardening the Organic Way*. London: Thorsons, 1983.

Philbrick, Helen, and Richard B. Gregg, *Companion Plants and How to Use Them*. London: Watkins, 1967.

Riotte, Louise, *Carrots Love Tomatoes: Secrets of Successful Companion Planting*. Pownal, VT: Storey Books, 1998.

Riotte, Louise, *Roses Love Garlic: Secrets of Companion Planting with Flowers*. Pownal, VT: Storey Books, 1998.

PERMACULTURE
Hart, Robert, *Forest Garden*. Devon: Green Books, 1991.

Mollison, Bill, *Introduction to Permaculture*. Tyalgum, NSW: Tagari Publications, 1994 (2nd ed.).

BIODYNAMICS
Corrin, George, *Handbook on Composting and the Biodynamic Preparations*. Clent: Biodynamic Agricultural Association, UK, 1995.

Pfeiffer, Ehrenfried, *Biodynamic Gardening and Farming (Vols 1–3)*. Spring Valley, MN: Mercury Press, 1983.

Philbrick, John, and Helen Philbrick, *Gardening for Health and Nutrition: An Introduction to the Method of Biodynamic Gardening*. Hudson, NY: Anthroposophic Press, 1971.

Steiner, Rudolf, *Agriculture*. (A course of lectures held at Koberwitz, Silesia, June 7 to June 16, 1924.) Biodynamic Farming and Gardening Assoc. Inc., USA, 1993.

TAO AND ECOSYSTEMS
Barrow, John D., *Theories of Everything: The Quest for Ultimate Explanation*. Oxford: Clarendon, 1991.

Coats, Callum, *Living Energies: An Exposition of the Concepts Related to the Theories of Viktor Schauberger*. Bath: Gateway, 1996.

Gauquelin, Michael, *The Cosmic Clocks*. London: Granada, 1973.

Goldsmith, Edward, *The Way: An Ecological World View*. Dartington: Themis Books, 1991.

Hart, Robert, *Beyond the Forest Garden*. London: Gaia Books Limited, 1996.

HRH The Prince of Wales, *The Lady Eve Balfour Memorial Lecture*, 1996. Soil Association, UK, 1996.

Lovelock, James, *Gaia: A New Look at Life on Earth*. Oxford: Oxford University Press, 1979.

Lovelock, James, *Gaia: The Practical Science of Planetary Medicine*. London: Gaia Books Limited, 1991.

Peat, David, *Blackfoot Physics: A Journey into the Native American Universe*. London: Fourth Estate, 1996.

Veith, Ilza (trans.), *The Yellow Emperor's Classic of Chinese Internal Medicine*. Berkeley, CA: University of California Press, 1972 (5th ed.).

FENG SHUI
Govert, Johndennis, *Feng Shui: Art and Harmony of Place*. Phoenix, AZ: Daikakuji Publications, 1993.

Lin, Jami, *Contemporary Earth Design: A Feng Shui Anthology*. Miami, FL: Earth Design, 1997.

Rossbach, Sarah, *Feng Shui: Ancient Chinese Wisdom on Arranging a Harmonious Living Environment*. London: Rider, 1991.

Walters, Derek, *The Feng Shui Handbook: A Practical Guide to Chinese Geomancy and Environmental Harmony*. London: Aquarian Press, 1991.

Wong, Eva, *Feng Shui: The Ancient Wisdom of Harmonious Living for Modern Times*. Boston, MA: Shambhala, 1996.

ORIENTAL GARDENS
Howard, Edwin J., *Chinese Garden Architecture: A Collection of Photographs of Minor Chinese Buildings*. New York, NY: Macmillan, 1931.

Rambach, Pierre and Suzanne Rambach, *Gardens of Longevity in China and Japan: The Art of the Stone Raisers*. New York, NY: Rizzoli International Publishers Ltd, 1987.

Yoshikawa, Isao, *Chinese Gardens of the Lower Yangtse River*. Toyko: Graphic-sha Publishing Company Ltd, 1990.

MOON AND PLANETARY PLANTING
Annual: Llewellyn's Organic Gardening Almanac. St. Paul, MN: Llewellyn Publications.

Annual: Llewellyn's 1997 Moon Sign Book and Lunar Gardening Guide. St. Paul, MN: Llewllyn Publications.

Annual: Moon Chart [showing the moon's phases and the dates and times it moves into each constellation]. From: Equinox, 78 Neal Street, Covent Garden, London, WC2H 9PA.

Annual: Raphael's Astronomical Ephemeris. Chippenham: W. Foulsham & Co. Ltd.

Annual: Thun, Maria, *Working with the Stars: A Biodynamic Sowing and Planting Calendar*. Launceston: Lanthorn Press.

Gower, J. R., *Gwydion's Planting Guide: The Definitive Moon-planting Manual*. Glastonbury: Pan Dimensional Collection, 1994.

Paungger, Johanna and Thomas Poppe, *Moon Time: The Art of Harmony with Nature and Lunar Cycles*. Saffron Walden: C. W. Daniel, 1995.

Riotte, Louise, *Planetary Planting*. San Diego, CA: Astro Computing Services, 1982. (Revised edition Pownal, VT: Storey Books, 1998).

Thun, Maria, *Work on the Land and the Constellations*. Launceston: Lanthorn Press, 1990.

GEOPATHIC STRESS
Gordon, Rolf, *Are You Sleeping in a Safe Place?* London: Dulwich Health Society, 1993 (5th ed.).

CHINESE PHILOSOPHY AND ASTROLOGY
Needham, Joseph, *Science and Civilisation in China*. Cambridge: Cambridge University Press, 1984.

Palmer, Martin et al, *T'ung Shu: The Ancient Chinese Almanac*. Kuala Lumpur: Vinpress, 1990.

I-CHING
Briggs, John, *Fractals: The Patterns of Chaos*. London: Thames & Hudson, 1982.

Capra, Fritjof, *The Tao of Physics: An Exploration of the Parallels Between Modern Physics and Eastern Mysticism*. London: Flamingo, 1993 (3rd ed.).

Ni, Hua-Ching, *The Book of Changes and Unchanging Truth*. Santa Monica, CA: Seven Star Communications, 1990 (2nd ed.).

Sterling, Marysol, *I Ching and Transpersonal Psychology*. York Beach, ME: Samuel Weiser, Inc., 1995.

Walter, Katya, *Tao of Chaos: Merging East and West*. Shaftesbury: Element, 1996.

Wilhelm, Richard, *I Ching or Book of Changes*. London: Arkana, 1989.

DOWSING
Davies, Rodney, *Dowsing*. London: Aquarian Press, 1991.

Ozaniec, Naomi, *Dowsing for Beginners*. London: Hodder & Stoughton, 1994.

Index

Acknowledgements

AUTHOR'S ACKNOWLEDGEMENTS

Firstly I should like to thank my long-suffering family for their patience and support. Next, Arto, for believing in me and enabling this to happen, and all the people who helped on my year-long search for the information I knew existed – but only in Chinese! Martin Palmer for the loan of his translation of the *T'ung Shu* and Rebecca Yeung from the University of Hong Kong Library for responding so promptly to a fax out of the blue. Alice and Mr Lee for introducing me to Professor Liu who so kindly translated that precious page. Val du Monceau and Kajal Sheth, who checked the text, for their constructive comments, and Sandra Thomas for her honesty. Thank you to all the fascinating teachers and wonderful "Feng Shui" friends I have met in the last few years and to all those who are striving to make the world a more harmonious place. Finally, I should like to thank Sue Minter for her plant table and help with plant names, and Pritty, Tessa and Zoë at Eddison Sadd, for gritting their teeth and putting up with me, and producing this book which 'evolved' right up to the deadline.

PICTURE CREDITS

T: TOP   B: BELOW   C: CENTRE   L: LEFT   R: RIGHT

J. Becker/Zefa 105L; Bridgeman Art Library: A Hong merchant's garden, Canton, Chinese School 10–11, Leonardo da Vinci, Galleria Dell' Accademia, Venice 13T, Private Collection 63; Linda Burgess/Garden Picture Library 79B; Nigel Cattlin/Holt Studios 37L; Liz Eddison 15R, 29T, 29B, 30B, 31R, 50, 61L, 76, 85B, 87B, 92R, 94L, 94R, 95R, 101T; E. T. Archive 47, 58; John Glover 27L, 28R, 51, 59T, 66, 68–9, 83, 85T, 92C, 110L, 111T; Jane Grushow/Zefa 106; Jerry Harpur 22, 26, 28L, 60, 61R, 79T, 80, 87T, 95L, 96L, 96R, 99, 100, 101B; Marcus Harper 93; Janos Jurka/Bruce Coleman Limited 33B; H. P. Merten/Zefa 111B; MJK/Photos Horticultural 110R; Needham Research Institute 40; Clive Nichols 13B, 15L, 23, 30, 46, 91, 92L, 98, 107; Photos Horticultural 49T, 103, 112, 116; Primrose Peacock/Holt Studios 37R; F. Rossotto/Zefa 97; Harry Smith Collection 49B; Ron Sutherland/Garden Picture Library 114; Juliette Wade 78, 102; Steven Wooster/Garden Picture Library 27R, 33B; Zefa 59B

EDDISON • SADD EDITIONS

Project Editors	Zoë Hughes & Tessa Monina
Proofreader	Nikky Twyman
Indexer	Dorothy Frame
Art Director	Elaine Partington
Art Editor	Pritty Ramjee
Illustrations	Julie Carpenter
Case Study Illustrations	Andrew Farmer
Illustrations (pages 46, 54)	Anthony Duke
Picture Researcher	Liz Eddison
Production	Charles James & Karyn Claridge

EDDISON SADD would like to thank Tinh Thong Nguyen of the An Tam Healing Centre, London, for supplying the Chinese calligraphy, and Rudolf Steiner Press for permission to use illustration reference for page 46 from *Work on the Land and the Constellations* by Maria Thun (Launceston: Lanthorn Press, 1990).